ARBEITSHEFT

A Workbook

for German

Grammar and

Communication

David M. Stillman, Ph.D.
Ronni L. Gordon, Ph.D.

with the assistance of
Raymond A. Phillips, Ph.D.
Muhlenberg College and Penn State University

 National Textbook Company
a division of NTC/CONTEMPORARY PUBLISHING GROUP
Lincolnwood, Illinois USA

Editorial Development: Mediatheque Publishers Services, Philadelphia, Pennsylvania

Illustrations: James Buckley

ISBN: 0-658-00954-0

CONTENTS

PREFACE

Arbeitsheft: A Workbook for German Grammar and Communication is designed to provide beginning and intermediate learners with the tools necessary to allow them to progress most effectively and efficiently in the mastery of German. Organized into 18 chapters, *Arbeitsheft* presents concise, structured **grammar explanations** with examples that reflect everyday usage, usually in the context of a brief conversation. The **exercises** in *Arbeitsheft* give learners of German ample practice with the basic structures usually covered by German textbooks at the beginning and intermediate levels. Most of the exercises are contextualized, thus inviting students to use their knowledge of German in engaging, communicative situations. **Vocabulary** items have been chosen to review and expand upon those presented in basal texts. When an exercise uses words and expressions not commonly found in textbooks, the words are presented and defined in a **vocabulary box** preceding the exercise. Some exercises in *Arbeitsheft* are built around **illustrations**. Students practice the grammar point in question by responding to these attractive visual cues.

The new German spelling rules affect relatively few of the words used in this book. The following are the most important:

- Combinations of noun + verb and verb + verb are now written separately. Thus, **Rad fahren** is now used instead of **radfahren,** and **spazieren gehen** is used instead of **spazierengehen.** Examples of both the old and new usage appear in *Arbeitsheft*.

- The letter **ß** is used now only after long vowels and diphthongs. After short vowels, **ss** is used: **muss, Hass, lässt, isst,** and so forth. Examples of both spellings appear in the workbook.

Arbeitsheft also highlights important features of the German-speaking world in the **culture boxes** that appear in all the chapters and that help create an authentic context for a particular exercise. Among the features presented in the culture boxes are the cities, food, sports, school systems, music and art, and industry of Germany, Austria, and Switzerland. Progressing from structured to self-expression exercises, *Arbeitsheft* offers **Und du?** and **Aufsätze** sections to encourage learners to use the grammatical structures and vocabulary they have studied to express their own ideas.

Students will find working through *Arbeitsheft* a rewarding learning experience because of its easy-to-follow format, the ample space provided to write answers, and the open and inviting design. Teachers will appreciate the flexible organization of *Arbeitsheft,* which allows them to select chapters in any order to reinforce the grammar points they are presenting or reviewing in their classes. The unique integration of all its features makes *Arbeitsheft* an engaging, user-friendly workbook that motivates learners to communicate and helps build real confidence in using German. The absolute integrity of content and format makes *Arbeitsheft* the perfect fit for any German textbook.

Personal Pronouns; *Sein*; The Definite Article and the Gender of Nouns; The Indefinite Article

I. Personal Pronouns; *Sein* to be

■ Study the conjugation of the verb **sein** (*to be*). Take careful note of the personal pronouns used with the verb forms.

	singular	plural
first person	ich **bin** *I am*	wir **sind** *we are*
second person	du **bist** *you are*	ihr **seid** *you are*
third person	er **ist** *he is* sie **ist** *she is* es **ist** *it is*	sie **sind** *they are* Sie **sind** *you are*

Notes:

1. Note that the same word (**sie**) is used for both *she* and *they* in German. However, the forms of the verb are different: **sie ist** *she is* vs. **sie sind** *they are*.

2. German has three words for **you**:

   Du is used to address one person with whom you are on a familiar or informal basis.

   Ihr is used to address two or more people with whom you are on a familiar or informal basis.

   Sie is used to address people with whom you are on a polite or formal basis.

3. Note that the forms for *they are* and *you* (formal) *are* are the same except that **Sie** is always capitalized when it means *you* (formal), regardless of its position in the sentence.

A. Wo sind sie? Tell where these people are, using the correct form of the present tense of the verb **sein.**

Beispiel   Johann / in Deutschland
           ➤ Johann ist in Deutschland.

1. Ursula / in Österreich

   _____

2. wir / in Berlin

   _____

3. ihr / in Europa

_____

4. ich / in Amerika

_____

5. Hans und Lotte / in Wien

_____

6. du / in New York

_____

7. Sie, Herr Professor, / hier

_____

8. Anton / in Hamburg

_____

B. Nummern. Study the numbers from one to twenty and write conversations about how old people are. Write out the numbers in your responses.

0	null	7	sieben	14	vierzehn
1	eins	8	acht	15	fünfzehn
2	zwei	9	neun	16	sechzehn
3	drei	10	zehn	17	siebzehn
4	vier	11	elf	18	achtzehn
5	fünf	12	zwölf	19	neunzehn
6	sechs	13	dreizehn	20	zwanzig

Beispiel   Peter / 16
➤ Wie alt ist Peter?
Er ist sechzehn.

1. Richard und Ulrich / 15

_____

_____

2. ihr / 13

_____

_____

3. dein Hund Roro / 4

_____

_____

4. Renate / 20

_____

_____

5. ihr / 17

_____

_____

6. du / ? / ?

_____

_____

Berlin und Wien

- After Germany's defeat in World War II, two German states were created. West Germany (**Bundesrepublik Deutschland**), composed of the British, American, and French occupation zones, had its capital in Bonn. The Soviet sector became East Germany (**Deutsche Demokratische Republik**), with its capital in East Berlin. East and West Germany were reunified in 1990 and Berlin again became the capital of Germany, although a few government departments will remain in Bonn. Berlin is located on the Spree River in northeastern Germany. It is a cosmopolitan and modern city, having been largely rebuilt after the war. Perhaps the best-known monument in Berlin is the **Brandenburger Tor** (The Brandenburg Gate). From this gate, people like to stroll on the famous boulevard called **Unter den Linden.** Berlin is known for its music, art, and theater. The **Pergamon Museum** is one of the most important museums of ancient history in the world. Berlin is the home of one of the greatest symphony orchestras in the world, the **Berlin Philharmonic.** Berlin also has a famous zoo, the **Zoologischer Garten.**
- **Wien** (Vienna), the capital of Austria, is located on the Danube River in the northeastern part of the country. A city full of history and monuments, Vienna can be seen from a boat ride on the Danube or by car tours around the **Ringstraße** (Ring Street), which circles the inner part of the city. Tourists enjoy the special ambience of Vienna with its elegant shops, pedestrian malls, cafés, and pastry shops. Of special interest are the **Hofburg** (the Habsburg Palace), home of the Habsburg emperors until 1918; the **Stephansdom** (St. Stephan's Cathedral), a Gothic cathedral; and the **Kunsthistorisches Museum,** one of the greatest art museums in the world. Vienna is a noted music center. The Vienna Philharmonic and the Vienna State Opera are world famous. Some of the greatest composers of all time lived and composed in Vienna: the Austrians Mozart, Haydn, Schubert, Bruckner, and Schoenberg, and the Germans Beethoven and Brahms. Vienna was the home of Johann Strauss, father, and his son, also named Johann, who composed some of the most famous waltzes and polkas ever written.

C. **Beschreiben wir!** (*Let's describe!*) Use the adjectives from the following list with the correct form of the present tense of **sein** to help Lise talk about her friends.

Beispiel   Manfred / klug
  ➤ Manfred ist klug.

Die Adjektive

faul *lazy*	**müde** *tired*
fleißig *hard-working*	**nett** *nice, pleasant*
froh *happy*	**traurig** *sad*
klug *intelligent, clever*	**zufrieden** *satisfied, happy*

1. Udo und Günter / faul

_____

2. Gregor / fleißig

_____

3. ich / müde

_____

4. wir / zufrieden

_____

5. ihr / traurig

_____

6. du / nett

_____

7. Markus und ich / froh

_____

II. The Definite Article and the Gender of Nouns

■   German nouns are divided into three classes or genders called *masculine,*
    feminine, and *neuter.* The gender is shown by the form of the definite article
    (*the* in English).

masculine	feminine
der Computer *computer*	**die Katze** *cat*
der Flughafen *airport*	**die Lehrerin** *(female) teacher*
der Hund *dog*	**die Schule** *school*
der Lehrer *teacher*	**die Uhr** *clock*

neuter

das Buch *book*

das Büro *office*

das Hotel *hotel*

das Telefon *telephone*

■ The pronoun **er** is used for all masculine nouns, whether referring to people or things. The pronoun **sie** is used for all feminine nouns, whether referring to people or things. The pronoun **es** is used only to refer to neuter nouns.

Wo ist der Flughafen?	*Where is the airport?*
Er ist weit weg.	*It's far away.*
Wie ist die Schule?	*What is the school like?*
Sie ist neu.	*It's new.*
Wie ist das Hotel?	*How is the hotel?*
Es ist bequem.	*It's comfortable.*

■ Some neuter nouns refer to people. These nouns are replaced by **es,** not by **er** or **sie.**

das Mädchen *girl*

das Kind *child*

Wo ist das Mädchen?	*Where is the girl?*
Es ist hier.	*She's here.*
Wo ist das Kind?	*Where is the child?*
Es ist da.	*He (she) is there.*

■ Note that all nouns begin with a capital letter in German no matter where they appear in the sentence.

D. Beschreiben wir! Write sentences describing these people and things by adding the definite article and the correct form of **sein.**

Beispiel Schule / neu
➤ Die Schule ist neu.

Beschreiben wir!

alt *old*	**interessant** *interesting*
neu *new*	**langweilig** *boring*
groß *big, large*	**schön** *beautiful*
klein *small*	**häßlich** *ugly*
breit *wide*	**modern** *modern*
schmal *narrow*	**kaputt** *broken, out of order*
hoch *high*	**riesig** *gigantic*
niedrig *low*	

---

1. Uhr / klein

   _____

2. Flughafen / modern

   _____

3. Lehrer / nett

   _____

4. Telefon / kaputt

   _____

5. Buch / interessant

   _____

6. Büro / groß

   _____

7. Katze / zufrieden

   _____

E. Stadtbesuch. *(Visiting the city.)* You're visiting a new city and need to ask for directions. Stop pedestrians to ask where each of the following places is, using **Wo ist** and the appropriate definite article and the noun given. Add **bitte** *(please)* for politeness.

Beispiel   Straße
➤ Wo ist die Mozartstraße, bitte?

Die Stadt (The city)

der Bahnhof *railroad station*	das Museum *museum*
die Bibliothek *library*	der Park *park*
die Brücke *bridge*	die Post *post office*
die Buchhandlung *bookstore*	das Rathaus *city hall*
der Dom *cathedral*	das Restaurant *restaurant*
das Geschäft *shop, store*	das Schwimmbad *swimming pool*
das Fußballstadion *soccer stadium*	der Sportplatz *playing field*
das Kaufhaus *department store*	die Straße *street*
das Kino *movie theater*	das Theater *theater*
der Kiosk *newsstand*	die Videothek *video store*
der Marktplatz *marketplace*	

---

1. Kaufhaus

   _____

2. Schwimmbad

   _____

3. Marktplatz

   _____

4. Restaurant

   _____

5. Videothek

   _____

6. Bahnhof

   _____

7. Museum

_____

8. Post

_____

F. Du beschreibst die Stadt. You've walked around the new city and are talking to a friend on the phone. Form sentences from the words given to describe what you have seen. Use the correct form of the definite article.

Beispiel Park / schön
    ➤ Der Park ist schön.

1. Rathaus / alt

_____

2. Fußballstadion / riesig

_____

3. Bibliothek / interessant

_____

4. Dom / hoch

_____

5. Geschäft / modern

_____

6. Kaufhaus / langweilig

_____

7. Brücke / schmal

_____

8. Kino / schön

_____

III. The Indefinite Article

■ Study the forms of the German indefinite article (English *a, an*).

masculine	feminine	neuter
ein Lehrer *a teacher*	eine Katze *a cat*	ein Buch *a book*
ein Flughafen *an airport*	eine Schule *a school*	ein Kind *a child*

G. Du besuchst eine Schule. You visited a friend's school. Make a list of what you saw there using the indefinite article.

Beispiel Sportplatz ➤ ein Sportplatz

1. Schwimmbad _____

2. Lehrer _____

3. Computer _____

4. Bibliothek _____

5. Telefon _____

6. Büro _____

7. Lehrerin _____

8. Katze _____

H. Du bist Reiseleiter(in). *(You're the tour guide.)* Pretend you are showing some friends around your city. Point out these places to them using the words given and the indefinite article.

Beispiel hier / Park
➤ Hier ist ein Park.

1. hier / Kaufhaus _____

2. dort / Buchhandlung _____

3. da / Museum _____

4. hier / Theater _____

5. da / Schule _____

6. dort / Hotel _____

7. hier / Kiosk   _____

8. dort / Fußballstadion   _____

I.   **Beschreibe die Stadt.** Look at the pictures below. Tell what each thing you see is and describe it by selecting one of the adjectives given.

Beispiel   groß / klein
       ➤ Das ist eine Buchhandlung.
          Die Buchhandlung ist groß.

1. schön / häßlich

    _____

    _____

2. alt / neu

    _____

    _____

➤➤➤➤➤➤

3. breit / schmal

_____

_____

4. hoch / niedrig

_____

_____

J. Und du? Answer the following questions in complete sentences.

1. Wie alt bist du?

_____

2. Wie alt ist dein Hund (deine Katze)?

_____

3. Bist du faul oder fleißig?

_____

4. Wie ist die Schule?

_____

5. Wie sind die Studenten?

_____

K. Aufsatz. Describe five of the following places in your area. Use the definite article, the correct form of **sein,** and an adjective.

Bibliothek	Park	Marktplatz
Buchhandlung	Museum	Flughafen
Fußballstadion	Rathaus	Restaurant
Schwimmbad	Bahnhof	Theater
Schule	Kino	Sportplatz

CHAPTER 2

Haben; Accusative Case (*Direct Object*); *Es gibt*

I. *Haben;* Expressions with *haben*

■ Study the conjugation of the verb **haben** *to have.*

	singular	plural
first person	ich **habe** *I have*	wir **haben** *we have*
second person	du **hast** *you have*	ihr **habt** *you have*
third person	er **hat** *he has* sie **hat** *she has* es **hat** *it has*	sie **haben** *they have* Sie **haben** *you have*

■ In some expressions, German uses **haben** + noun where English uses *to be* + adjective:

Hunger haben *to be hungry*

Durst haben *to be thirsty*

Angst haben *to be afraid*

Heimweh haben *to be homesick*

■ In other expressions, German differs from English by omitting the article in front of the noun.

Kopfschmerzen haben *to have a headache*

Bauchschmerzen haben *to have a stomachache*

Schnupfen haben *to have a cold*

A. Ausdrücke mit *haben.* (*Expressions with* haben.) Write sentences about what these people are feeling or what conditions they have, using the correct form of **haben.**

Beispiel   Jürgen / Hunger
➤ Jürgen hat Hunger.

1. Monika / Durst   _____

2. Wilhelm / Angst   _____

3. ich / Schnupfen   _____

4. wir / Bauchschmerzen   _____

5. ihr / Hunger   _____

6. du / Kopfschmerzen   _____

7. Ulrike und Jutta / Heimweh   _____

II. Accusative Case (Direct Object)

■ German has four cases: nominative, genitive, dative, and accusative. Cases show the role of a noun in the sentence. The nominative case labels the subject of the sentence. The forms you have seen so far are nominatives. The accusative labels the direct object of the verb. If a noun is the direct object of the verb, the masculine definite article **der** becomes **den** and the masculine indefinite article **ein** becomes **einen**. The feminine and neuter articles remain the same. Compare the forms of the nominative and accusative.

nominative	accusative
der Bleistift, ein Bleistift	**den Bleistift, einen Bleistift**
die Schule, eine Schule	**die Schule, eine Schule**
das Buch, ein Buch	**das Buch, ein Buch**

Der Bleistift ist nicht hier. Hast du den Bleistift?	*The pencil isn't here. Do you have the pencil?*
Haben Sie einen Computer? Ja, und wir haben auch einen Kopierer.	*Do you have a computer? Yes, and we have a photocopier, too.*

B. Was haben wir? What do people have for their work at school? Form sentences with the correct form of **haben,** the noun, and the appropriate indefinite article.

Schulsachen (School supplies)

der Block *pad of paper*	**der Leuchtstift** *highlighter*
der Computer *computer*	**das Lineal** *ruler*
die Diskette *diskette*	**der Radiergummi** *eraser*
der Drucker *printer*	**die Schultasche** *school bag*
der Kugelschreiber *ballpoint pen*	**der Taschenrechner** *calculator*

Beispiel   Ulrich / Computer
➢ Ulrich hat einen Computer.

1. ich / Block

   _____

2. du / Kugelschreiber

   _____

3. der Lehrer / Lineal

   _____

4. Monika und Friedrich / Radiergummi

_____

5. wir / Taschenrechner

_____

6. die Klasse / Drucker

_____

7. ihr / Leuchtstift

_____

8. Klaus / Schultasche

_____

9. wir / Diskette

_____

Ausbildung (Education)

- All children in Germany are required to attend school between the ages of 6 and 16. The first four years of school, consisting of basic classes, are called **die Grundschule.** Then students may choose from **die Hauptschule,** which prepares students for jobs in trade and industry; **die Realschule,** which prepares students for mid-level positions in business or public service; **Gymnasium,** which teaches academics, preparing students for university and higher level positions in business; and **die Gesamtschule,** which combines the three other kinds of high schools.
- After the seven- to nine-year **Gymnasium** curriculum, students take the **Abitur,** a series of tests given to determine the college or university they will attend or the position for which they will be suited.

C. Wer hat die Dinge? Ulrich has found out who has the missing classroom supplies. Use the correct form of **haben** + definite article + noun to express what he says.

Beispiel   Trudi / Leuchtstift
         ➤ Trudi hat den Leuchtstift.

1. Bärbel und Karl / Drucker

   _____

2. du / Taschenrechner

   _____

3. ihr / Computer

   _____

4. die Lehrerin / Diskette

   _____

5. ich / Radiergummi

   _____

6. wir / Schultasche

   _____

7. Sie / Kugelschreiber

   _____

8. ihr / Block

   _____

9. Franz / Lineal

   _____

D. Wo sind die Dinge? Write conversations in which one person asks where certain things are and the other answers that he or she has them, but that they are over there—**dort drüben.**

Beispiel Kugelschreiber
    ➤ Wo ist der Kugelschreiber?
      Ich habe den Kugelschreiber. Er ist dort drüben.

1. Lineal

2. Diskette

3. Leuchtstift

4. Taschenrechner

5. Block

6. Schultasche

III. *Es gibt*

- The expression **es gibt** means *there is* and *there are* and is always followed by the accusative. The question form is **gibt es** + accusative.

Gibt es hier einen Computer?   *Is there a computer here?*
Ja, es gibt hier einen Computer   *Yes, there is a computer here and also*
   und einen Drucker.   *a printer.*

E. Richtungsangaben. *(Giving directions.)* Write conversations about places in a city. The first person asks if there is such a place. The second tells him or her where it is.

Beispiel   Park / dort drüben
          ➤ Gibt es hier einen Park?
             Ja, der Park ist dort drüben.

Richtungen (Directions)

dort drüben *over there*	**links** *to the left*
dort unten *down there*	**nicht weit** *not far*
gegenüber *across the way, opposite*	**rechts** *to the right*
geradeaus *straight ahead*	**um die Ecke** *around the corner*
in der Nähe *nearby*	**weit weg** *far away*
irgendwo hier *somewhere around here*	

---

1. Bibliothek / dort um die Ecke

   _____

   _____

2. Fußballstadion / rechts

   _____

   _____

3. Kaufhaus / geradeaus

   _____

   _____

➤➤➤➤➤

4. Dom / hier links

_____

_____

5. Marktplatz / nicht weit weg

_____

_____

6. Museum / hier in der Nähe

_____

_____

7. Schwimmbad / irgendwo hier

_____

_____

F. Einem Freund die Stadt zeigen. *(Showing a friend around the city.)*
Pretend you are showing a German friend around the city. Use **es gibt** with the expression of location indicated to tell him or her where the following places are.

Beispiel Schule / dort drüben
➢ Es gibt dort drüben eine Schule.

1. Flughafen / dort drüben

_____

2. Kino / gegenüber der Schule

_____

3. Bahnhof / hier in der Nähe

_____

4. Park / rechts

_____

5. Hotel / um die Ecke

_____

6. Kaufhaus / irgendwo hier

_____

7. Bibliothek / hier links

_____

8. Schwimmbad / dort unten

_____

G. In der Schule. Create conversations between two young people talking about school. The first, using **gibt es,** asks the second if his or her school has certain things. The second, using **haben,** answers in each case that they have them.

Beispiel   Schwimmbad
       ➤ Gibt es ein Schwimmbad?
         Ja, wir haben ein Schwimmbad.

In der Schule	
der Hörsaal _lecture hall_	**der Schulhof** _schoolyard, playground_
das Labor _laboratory_	**das Sekretariat** _school office_
das Lehrerzimmer _staff room_	**das Stadion** _stadium_
die Mensa _cafeteria_	**die Turnhalle** _gymnasium_

1. Sekretariat

_____

_____

2. Labor

_____

_____

3. Schulhof

_____

_____

➤➤➤➤➤

4. Turnhalle

_____

_____

5. Hörsaal

_____

_____

6. Lehrerzimmer

_____

_____

7. Stadion

_____

_____

8. Mensa

_____

_____

H. Was gibt es? Using **es gibt,** make a list of five things you have in your desk
or bookbag.

1. _____

2. _____

3. _____

4. _____

5. _____

I. Und du? Answer the following questions in complete sentences.

1. Was hast du heute?

    _____

2. Hast du einen Computer?

    _____

3. Wie ist der Computer?

    _____

4. Gibt es hier einen Kiosk?

    _____

5. Wo ist die Videothek?

    _____

J. Aufsatz. Pretend you are showing a German friend around your school and neighborhood. Point out at least six things to your visitor, using **es gibt** or **haben** and a phrase showing location.

Present Tense of Verbs;
Present Tense of Strong Verbs

I. Present Tense of Verbs

- The infinitive of German verbs ends in **-en**: **kaufen** (English: *to buy*). As you have seen with **sein** and **haben,** German verbs change their forms according to the subject and tense. Regular verbs add endings to the stem for each person in the conjugation. The stem of a German verb is formed by dropping the infinitive ending **-en.**

KAUFEN *TO BUY* (stem: *kauf-*)

	singular	plural
first person	ich **kaufe**	wir **kaufen**
second person	du **kaufst**	ihr **kauft**
third person	er/sie/es **kauft**	sie/Sie **kaufen**

Regular verbs are called weak verbs in German grammar. Here are some common weak verbs:

besuchen *to visit*	**lachen** *to laugh*	**suchen** *to look for*
brauchen *to need*	**leben** *to live (be alive)*	**weinen** *to cry*
hoffen *to hope*	**machen** *to make*	**wohnen** *to live (reside)*
holen *to get*	**sagen** *to say*	**zahlen** *to pay*
hören *to hear*	**spielen** *to play*	

A. Wer? Match each of the following subjects with the letter of its appropriate verb form. If some subjects can be used with more than one verb form, indicate all possibilities.

_____ 1. du   a. lachen

_____ 2. Sie   b. brauche

_____ 3. Heinrich   c. wohnst

_____ 4. Susi und Bärbel   d. weint

_____ 5. ich   e. besucht

_____ 6. ihr   f. hoffen

_____ 7. wir

B. Welches Subjekt? Check all of the possible subjects with which the verb forms can be used.

1. besuche

   ich ___ du ___ er ___ wir ___ ihr ___ Franz und Monika ___ Sie ___

2. macht

   ich ___ du ___ er ___ wir ___ ihr ___ Franz und Monika ___ Sie ___

3. leben

   ich ___ du ___ er ___ wir ___ ihr ___ Franz und Monika ___ Sie ___

4. zahlst

   ich ___ du ___ er ___ wir ___ ihr ___ Franz und Monika ___ Sie ___

5. spiele

   ich ___ du ___ er ___ wir ___ ihr ___ Franz und Monika ___ Sie ___

6. sucht

   ich ___ du ___ er ___ wir ___ ihr ___ Franz und Monika ___ Sie ___

7. sagen

   ich ___ du ___ er ___ wir ___ ihr ___ Franz und Monika ___ Sie ___

8. holst

   ich ___ du ___ er ___ wir ___ ihr ___ Franz und Monika ___ Sie ___

C. Der Fremdenverkehr. *(Tourism.)* Compose sentences with the correct form of **besuchen** and the elements given to tell what these people are visiting during their stay in a German city.

Beispiel Jürgen / Museum
   ➢ Jürgen besucht das Museum.

1. Ursula und Wilhelm / Dom

   _____

2. ich / Bibliothek

   _____

3. du / Kaufhaus

   _____

➣➣➣➣➣

4. Erich / Park

_____

5. wir / Marktplatz

_____

6. ihr / Rathaus

_____

7. ich / Fußballstadion

_____

8. die Lehrerin / Schule

_____

D. Wo wohnen Manfreds Freunde? Manfred is describing where in Germany, Austria, and Switzerland he and his friends live. Use the verb **wohnen** to write what he says.

Beispiel Ingrid / Berlin
➤ Ingrid wohnt in Berlin.

1. ich / Frankfurt

_____

2. ihr / Hamburg

_____

3. Karl und Robert / Wien

_____

4. du / Bern

_____

5. wir / München

_____

6. Erika / Zürich

_____

7. Sie / Salzburg

_____

8. Anton / Köln

_____

Die deutsche Wirtschaft (The German economy)

- After World War II, the German economy was in ruins. In West Germany, the economic and democratic policies of Chancellor Konrad Adenauer, the aid provided by the United States through the Marshall Plan, and the resourcefulness of the Germans led to rapid economic growth. Today, Germany is the third largest economy in the world. Its leading industries include iron, steel, coal, cement, chemicals, machinery, vehicles, ships, electronics, food, and beverages.
- Frankfurt am Main (on the Main River) in central Germany is the financial capital of the country. This modern city is home to the German stock exchange and major banks, and is also an important scientific research and cultural center. An important international book fair is held annually in Frankfurt.
- Hamburg, Germany's main port, is a rich industrial and commercial center. It is located on the Elbe River, which empties into the North Sea. Visitors get a fine view of the city, including its famous copper towers, if they take a boat ride on the Elbe. The composer Johannes Brahms was born in Hamburg in 1833.

E. Schulsachen. *(School supplies.)* Use the verb **brauchen** to tell what the following people need for the new school year.

Beispiel Irmgard / Bleistift
➤ Irmgard braucht einen Bleistift.

1. Sabine und Ursula / Block

_____

2. der Lehrer / Diskette

_____

3. der Student / Kugelschreiber

_____

➤➤➤➤➤

4. ich / Drucker

_____

5. du / Radiergummi

_____

6. ihr / Computer

_____

7. Franz / Schultasche

_____

8. wir / Taschenrechner

_____

F. Erster Tag in der Schule. Use the verb **suchen** to tell what the following people are looking for on their first day at **Gymnasium.**

Beispiel Lehrerin / Klasse
➤ Die Lehrerin sucht die Klasse.

1. wir / Turnhalle

_____

2. Lehrer / Lehrerzimmer

_____

3. Sebastian und Bernd / Schwimmbad

_____

4. du / Sekretariat

_____

5. ihr / Hörsaal

_____

6. Frau Bergmann / Labor

_____

7. Monika und Alfred / Bibliothek

_____

8. ich / Mensa

_____

II. Present Tense of Strong Verbs

- Strong verbs in German show changes in the vowel of the stem in some of their forms. Some of these verbs have vowel changes in the **du** and the **er/sie/es** forms of the present tense.

SPRECHEN _TO SPEAK_ (change: **e > i**)

	singular	plural
first person	ich **spreche**	wir **sprechen**
second person	du **sprichst**	ihr **sprecht**
third person	er/sie/es **spricht**	sie/Sie **sprechen**

Other verbs like **sprechen:**

essen _to eat:_ ich esse, du ißt, er ißt

geben _to give:_ ich gebe, du gibst, er gibt

helfen _to help:_ ich helfe, du hilfst, er hilft

nehmen _to take:_ ich nehme, du nimmst, er nimmt

FALLEN _TO FALL_ (change: **a > ä**)

	singular	plural
first person	ich **falle**	wir **fallen**
second person	du **fällst**	ihr **fallt**
third person	er/sie/es **fällt**	sie/Sie **fallen**

Other verbs like **fallen:**

fahren _to ride, drive:_ ich fahre, du fährst, er fährt

lassen _to let, allow:_ ich lasse, du läßt, er läßt (**verlassen** _to leave, abandon_ is conjugated like **lassen**)

schlafen _to sleep:_ ich schlafe, du schläfst, er schläft

tragen _to wear, carry:_ ich trage, du trägst, er trägt

LESEN *TO READ* (change: **e > ie**)

	singular	plural
first person	ich **lese**	wir **lesen**
second person	du **liest**	ihr **lest**
third person	er/sie/es **liest**	sie/Sie **lesen**

Another verb like **lesen**:

sehen *to see:* **ich sehe, du siehst, er sieht**

LAUFEN *TO RUN, WALK* (change: **au > äu**)

	singular	plural
first person	ich **laufe**	wir **laufen**
second person	du **läufst**	ihr **lauft**
third person	er/sie/es **läuft**	sie/Sie **laufen**

G. Was spricht man? Tell what languages the following people speak using the verb **sprechen**.

Beispiel   wir / Deutsch
         ➢ Wir sprechen Deutsch.

Sprachen (Languages)

Chinesisch *Chinese*	**Italienisch** *Italian*
Deutsch *German*	**Japanisch** *Japanese*
Englisch *English*	**Russisch** *Russian*
Französisch *French*	**Spanisch** *Spanish*

1. Mario und Luis / Spanisch

_____

2. Shu Ling / Chinesisch

_____

3. ihr / Russisch

_____

4. Noriko / Japanisch

_____

5. du / Englisch

_____

6. wir / Französisch

_____

7. ich / Italienisch

_____

8. Dieter / Deutsch

_____

H. Alle lesen. *(Everyone's reading.)* Tell what the following people are reading, using the correct form of the verb **lesen.**

Beispiel   ich / Buch
        ➢ Ich lese ein Buch.

Lesestoff (Reading material)	
der Artikel *article*	**das Märchen** *fairy tale*
der Bericht *report*	**der Roman** *novel*
die Erzählung *story*	**die Zeitschrift** *magazine*
das Gedicht *poem*	**die Zeitung** *newspaper*

1. der Lehrer / Artikel

_____

2. Markus und Peter / Zeitschrift

_____

3. ich / Roman

_____

4. das Kind / Märchen

_____

5. ihr / Erzählung

_____

➢➢➢➢➢

6. der Student / Gedicht

_____

7. du / Bericht

_____

8. wir / Zeitung

_____

I. Alle fahren irgendwohin. *(Everybody's going somewhere.)* Tell where the following people are traveling to, using the verb **fahren** and the preposition **nach.**

Beispiel   wir / Berlin
    ➢ Wir fahren nach Berlin.

1. du / Wien

_____

2. Johann / London

_____

3. Inge und Fritz / New York

_____

4. der Lehrer / Zürich

_____

5. ihr / San Francisco

_____

6. Monika / Montreal

_____

7. die Studentin / Hamburg

_____

8. ich / Chicago

_____

J. Und du? Answer the following questions in complete sentences.

1. Sprichst du, wenn der Lehrer spricht?

_____

2. Was liest du?

_____

3. Was sprecht ihr zu Hause (*at home*)? Englisch? Deutsch?

_____

4. Was brauchst du? Einen Kugelschreiber? Eine Diskette?

_____

5. Wohnst du weit weg oder in der Nähe?

_____

K. Aufsatz. Describe a typical scene among you and your friends or you and your family. Tell what each person is doing.

CHAPTER 4

Present Tense of Verbs Whose Stem Ends in -t or -d;
Other Irregularities in the Conjugation of
*the Present Tense; Negation with **nicht** and **kein**;*
*Use of **gern**; Use of **lieber** and **am liebsten***

I. Present Tense of Verbs Whose Stem Ends in *-t* or *-d*

- Verbs whose stem ends in -t or -d, such as **antworten** *to answer* or **schneiden** *to cut,* insert an -e before the endings of the **du, er,** and **ihr** forms.

ANTWORTEN *TO ANSWER* (stem: *antwort-*)

	singular	plural
first person	ich **antworte**	wir **antworten**
second person	du **antwortest**	ihr **antwortet**
third person	er/sie/es **antwortet**	sie/Sie **antworten**

SCHNEIDEN *TO CUT* (stem: *schneid-*)

	singular	plural
first person	ich **schneide**	wir **schneiden**
second person	du **schneidest**	ihr **schneidet**
third person	er/sie/es **schneidet**	sie/Sie **schneiden**

- Verbs whose stem ends in **-n** preceded by a consonant add **-e** in the same forms as **antworten** and **schneiden.**

RECHNEN *TO CALCULATE, COMPUTE* (stem: *rechn-*)

	singular	plural
first person	ich **rechne**	wir **rechnen**
second person	du **rechnest**	ihr **rechnet**
third person	er/sie/es **rechnet**	sie/Sie **rechnen**

- Some verbs whose stem ends in **-t** or **-d** and some verbs whose stem ends in **-n** preceded by a consonant add **-e** in the same forms as **antworten** and **schneiden.**

arbeiten *to work*

beantworten eine Frage *to answer a question*

binden *to tie:* **einen Knoten binden** *to tie a knot*

öffnen *to open*

reden *to speak, talk*

warten *to wait*

zeichnen *to draw*

A. Das Präsens. *(Present tense.)* Complete the following sentences with the correct form of the verb in parentheses.

1. (antworten)   Die Studenten fragen und der Lehrer _____.

2. (öffnen)   Du _____ die Tür.

3. (warten)   Hans _____ unten.

4. (zeichnen)   Susi _____ (ein Haus).

5. (binden)   Das Kind _____ einen Knoten.

6. (rechnen)   Ihr _____ mit einem Taschenrechner.

7. (reden)   Ihr _____ mit Friedrich und Margarete.

8. (beantworten)   Du _____ die Frage.

9. (schneiden)   Mutter _____ das Brot.

10. (arbeiten)   Vater _____ hier in der Nähe.

B. Auch. *(Also.)* Tell that the following people do these things too.

Beispiel   Wir spielen. (Karl und Peter)
➤ Karl und Peter spielen auch.

1. Wir warten schon lange. (Bärbel)

_____

2. Sie antworten. (Du)

_____

3. Ich zeichne mit Kreide. (Das Kind)

_____

4. Wir rechnen schnell. (Der Lehrer)

_____

5. Ich schneide den Käse. (Mutti)

_____

➤➤➤➤➤

6. Wir reden mit Paul. (Ihr)

_____

7. Sie binden einen Knoten. (Du)

_____

8. Ich beantworte die Frage. (Ihr)

_____

C. Frag *wer* macht das. Pretend you didn't hear who is doing these things. In each case, ask who is performing the action using **wer** and the third-person singular form of the verb.

Beispiel   Hedda und ich arbeiten.
➤ Wer arbeitet?

1. Hans und Ulrich zeichnen gut.

_____

2. Wir schneiden das Blatt Papier in Stücke.

_____

3. Die Kinder öffnen die Tür.

_____

4. Die Studenten rechnen mit einem Taschenrechner.

_____

5. Vati und Mutti reden mit Stefan.

_____

6. Marie und Kurt beantworten die Frage.

_____

7. Wir binden einen Knoten.

_____

8. Jutta und Andreas warten dort unten.

_____

II. Other Irregularities in the Conjugation of the Present Tense

- Verbs with stems ending in -s, -ß, or -z add only -t, not -st, in the **du** form.

grüßen	du **grüßt**
lesen	du **liest**
verlassen	du **verläßt**

Verbs with stems ending in -s, -ß, or -z:

beißen *to bite*	**putzen** *to clean*
essen (e > i) (**du/er ißt**) *to eat*	**schließen** *to close*
gießen *to water*	**sitzen** *to sit*
grüßen *to greet, say hello to*	**stoßen** *to push*
heißen *to be called, to be named*	**tanzen** *to dance*
lassen (a > ä) *to let*	**vergessen** (e > i) *to forget*
lesen (e > ie) *to read*	**verlassen** (a > ä) *to leave*
müssen (**du mußt**) *must, to have to*	

Note the present tense of **wissen** *to know:*

	singular	plural
first person	ich **weiß**	wir **wissen**
second person	du **weißt**	ihr **wißt**
third person	er/sie/es **weiß**	sie/Sie **wissen**

- Verbs with stems ending in -**el** or -**er** add only -**n,** not -**en,** in the infinitive and in the **wir** and **sie** (plural) forms:

sammeln *to collect:* **wir/sie sammeln**

ändern *to change:* **wir/sie ändern**

Some verbs with stems ending in -**el** or -**er**:

angeln *to fish*	**lächeln** *to smile*
bedauern *to regret, be sorry about*	**plaudern** *to chat*
bezweifeln *to doubt*	**rudern** *to row*
bügeln *to iron*	**segeln** *to sail*
füttern *to feed*	**wandern** *to hike*
klingeln *to ring*	**wechseln** *to change (money)*

D. Zu Hause. *(At home.)* Ask a new friend questions about what he or she does at home. Use the **du** form.

Beispiel mit deinen Freunden plaudern
➤ Plauderst du mit deinen Freunden?

Vokabular

die Blume *flower*

die Briefmarke (plural: **die Briefmarken**) *(postage) stamp*

das Fenster (plural: **die Fenster**) *window*

die Kleider (plural) *clothing*

der Nachbar *neighbor*

das Zimmer room

---

1. dein Zimmer putzen

   _____

2. die Blumen gießen

   _____

3. die Fenster schließen

   _____

4. die Zeitung lesen

   _____

5. die Kleider bügeln

   _____

6. die Katze füttern

   _____

7. deine Nachbarn grüßen

   _____

8. Briefmarken sammeln

   _____

Arbeitsheft: A Workbook for German Grammar and Communication

E. Urlaub. *(Vacation.)* Create conversations in which a student asks a group of friends about what they do on vacation. Use the **ihr** form in the questions and the **wir** form in the answers.

Beispiel   tanzen
        ➢ Tanzt ihr?
           Ja, wir tanzen.

1. die Stadt verlassen

   _____

2. wandern

   _____

3. mit Freunden plaudern

   _____

4. Bücher lesen

   _____

5. angeln

   _____

6. rudern

   _____

7. segeln

   _____

8. mit vielen Menschen reden

   _____

III. Negation with *nicht* and *kein*

■ Verbs in German are made negative by placing the word **nicht** after them.

Johann tanzt nicht.	*Johann doesn't dance.*
Wo wohnt er?	*Where does he live?*
Ich weiß nicht.	*I don't know.*

■ **Nicht** comes after the noun that is the object of the verb it negates.

Wir besuchen den Marktplatz nicht.	*We're not visiting the marketplace.*
Ihr lest den Artikel nicht.	*You're not reading the article.*

■ Prepositional phrases such as **in der Nähe,** expressions of location such as **gegenüber,** and adjectives usually follow **nicht.**

Die Schule ist nicht in der Nähe.	*The school is not nearby.*
Die Schule ist nicht dort drüben.	*The school is not over there.*
Die Schule ist nicht modern.	*The school is not modern.*

■ **Kein** negates nouns. It has the same forms as the indefinite article **ein,** so the masculine accusative form is **keinen. Kein** and **nicht** do not appear together.

Ich kaufe kein Buch.	*I'm not buying any book.*
Wir haben keinen Taschenrechner.	*We do not have a calculator.*

F. Das machen sie nicht. Answer each question in the negative using **nicht.**

Beispiel   Tanzt du?
> ➤ Nein, ich tanze nicht.

1. Ist das Geschäft geradeaus?

   _____

2. Ist das Stadion riesig?

   _____

3. Bügelt sie die Kleider?

   _____

4. Redet ihr mit den Freunden?

   _____

5. Ist das Kino um die Ecke?

   _____

6. Vergißt du die Bücher?

_____

7. Wartet ihr dort unten?

_____

8. Putzt du dein Zimmer?

_____

G. Ohne Schulbedarf. *(Without school supplies.)* These students are all missing some important school supplies. Use **haben** and **kein** to tell what they don't have.

Beispiel Gisela / Bleistift
  ➢ Gisela hat keinen Bleistift.

1. Georg / Lineal

_____

2. Birgit / Diskette

_____

3. die Lehrerin / Papier

_____

4. Erik und Karin / Leuchtstift

_____

5. ich / Drucker

_____

6. wir / Kugelschreiber

_____

7. ihr / Taschenrechner

_____

8. du / Schultasche

_____

H. Eine langweilige Stadt. *(A boring city.)* You're visiting a friend in the small town where he lives. You ask him if the town has certain attractions. He answers in each case that it doesn't. Write your exchanges using **es gibt + kein.** Remember that **es gibt** is followed by the accusative.

Beispiel   Kaufhaus
  ➤ Gibt es hier ein Kaufhaus?
    Nein, es gibt kein Kaufhaus.

1. Stadion

_____

_____

2. Marktplatz

_____

_____

3. Bibliothek

_____

_____

4. Universität

_____

_____

5. Dom

_____

_____

6. Schwimmbad

_____

_____

7. Park

_____

_____

8. Museum

_____

_____

IV. Use of *gern*

- To express the idea of liking someone or something, German uses the adverb **gern** after the appropriate verb.

  To say you like someone, use **gern haben**:

Ich habe Monika gern.	*I like Monica.*
Wir haben den Lehrer gern.	*We like the teacher.*

  To express what you like to eat and drink, use **gern** with **essen** and **trinken**.

Ich esse gern Eis.	*I like ice cream.*
Du trinkst gern Tee.	*You like tea.*

  To express what people like to do, add **gern** after any verb.

Die Studentin schreibt gern.	*The student likes to write.*
Wir spielen gern Schach.	*We like to play chess.*

- To express dislikes, add **nicht** before **gern**.

Wir haben den Nachbar nicht gern.	*We don't like the neighbor.*
Das Kind ißt nicht gern Gemüse.	*The child doesn't like to eat vegetables.*

I. **Was essen sie gern?** Frau Müller is talking about what members of her family like to eat and drink. Write out what she says using **gern essen/ trinken.**

Beispiel Großmutter / Gemüse
➢ Großmutter ißt gern Gemüse.

Die Familie (The family)

das Baby *baby*	**die Mutter** *mother*
die Frau *wife*	**der Onkel** *uncle*
die Großmutter *grandmother*	**der Sohn** *son*
der Großvater *grandfather*	**die Tante** *aunt*
die Kinder *children* (plural)	**die Tochter** *daughter*
die Kusine *(female) cousin*	**der Vater** *father*
der Mann *husband*	**der Vetter** *(male) cousin*

Speisen und Getränke (Food and drink)

die Bonbons (plural) *candy*	**der Orangensaft** *orange juice*
das Brot *bread*	**die Pizza** *pizza*
das Eis *ice cream*	**das Schnitzel** *breaded cutlet* (pl. **die Schnitzel**)
der Kaffee *coffee*	**der Tee** *tea*
der Käse *cheese*	**die Wurst** *sausage*
die Limonade *lemonade, soft drink*	
die Milch *milk*	

---

1. meine Tochter / Orangensaft

   _____

2. Großvater und Großmutter / Tee

   _____

3. mein Sohn / Pizza

   _____

4. mein Mann / Wurst

   _____

5. ich / Brot

_____

6. Onkel Karl / Kaffee

_____

7. Tante Gerda / Limonade

_____

8. die Kinder / Eis

_____

9. das Baby / Milch

_____

10. mein Vetter und meine Kusine / Bonbons

_____

Das Essen (food)

- The traditional hearty German fare, with its sausages, pig's knuckles, and cabbage, or **Kraut,** has been replaced by an international, multicultural cuisine during the last few decades. Germany has become a country of immigrants and of many diverse cultures. When choosing a restaurant, Germans are more likely to seek out one offering Japanese, Chinese, Greek, or Turkish specialties than German food. However, **Wiener Schnitzel,** a thin breaded pork or veal cutlet fried in butter, remains a favorite.
- The **Kartoffel** (potato), brought from the New World to Germany in the 16th century, became the favorite vegetable of the Germans. Potatoes are served boiled, mashed, pan fried, or French fried. **Kartoffelpuffer** (potato pancakes) are served with **Apfelmuß** (applesauce). Potatoes are the preferred side dish in the northern and southeastern parts of Germany, while noodles are more popular in the southwest. Flat egg noodles and **Spätzle** _(little sparrows)_, a hearty little homemade noodle, are favorites.
- In recent years, regional cuisine has enjoyed a renaissance, even among young people. Regional cuisine is influenced by geography. The states that border France—Baden-Württemberg and the Saarland—are influenced by French cuisine, and seafood is dominant in the northern coastal regions that border the North Sea and the Baltic Sea.
- And, of course, nowadays there's always McDonald's—wherever you go.

J. Alle haben Urlaub! *(Everyone has a vacation!)* Tell what these people like to do on vacation using the word **gern.**

Beispiel   Roswitha / lesen
➢ Roswitha liest gern.

1. die Lehrerin / schreiben

   _____

2. du / segeln

   _____

3. wir / wandern

   _____

4. ihr / plaudern

   _____

5. du / tanzen

   _____

6. Markus / zeichnen

   _____

7. ich / rudern

   _____

8. mein Vater und mein Onkel / angeln

   _____

V. Use of *lieber* and *am liebsten*

■ To express what people like to do better, replace **gern** with **lieber:**

Wir rudern gern, aber wir schwimmen lieber.	*We like to row, but we prefer swimming.*

■ To express what people like to do best, replace **gern** with **am liebsten:**

Mein Vater angelt am liebsten.	*My father likes fishing best.*

K. Was tun sie lieber? Create conversations about what these people like to do. Use **gern** in the question, but **lieber** in the answer. Change nouns to pronouns in your answers.

Beispiel Bärbel / schwimmen / tanzen
      ➤ Schwimmt Bärbel gern?
        Ja, aber sie tanzt lieber.

1. Hans / Gemüse essen / Bonbons essen

    _____

    _____

2. Karl und Ulrich / angeln / wandern

    _____

    _____

3. Jutta / Zeitungen lesen / Zeitschriften lesen

    _____

    _____

4. ihr / Fußball spielen / Schach spielen

    _____

    _____

5. Tante Gerda / lesen / plaudern

    _____

    _____

6. Martin / studieren / Briefmarken sammeln

    _____

    _____

7. du / ? / ?

    _____

    _____

L. Das tun sie am liebsten. Tell what the following people like to do best on the weekends.

Beispiel Christa / tanzen
> ➤ Christa tanzt am liebsten.

1. Elke und Marie / wandern

   _____

2. Helmut / zeichnen

   _____

3. du / lesen

   _____

4. ihr / Schach spielen

   _____

5. Großvater / angeln

   _____

6. ich / segeln

   _____

7. Joachim / schlafen

   _____

8. wir / Fußball spielen

   _____

M. Und du? Answer the following questions in complete sentences.

1. Was ißt du am liebsten?

   _____

2. Was trinkst du lieber? Orangensaft oder Limonade?

   _____

3. Was tust du am liebsten, wenn du Urlaub hast?

   _____

4. Tanzt du gern? Liest du gern?

   _____

5. Was ißt du lieber? Eis oder Bonbons?

   _____

N. Aufsatz. Write a paragraph of five sentences about a day that you are
spending in the country with family and/or friends. What do you and
the people with you like to do? What are your and their favorite activities?
What do you and they not like? What foods do you and they like to eat?

Word Order: Verb in Second Position; Yes/No Questions; Use of *man*

I. Word Order: Verb in Second Position

■ In a simple sentence in German, the second element is always the verb.

Wir schwimmen heute.	*We're (going) swimming today.*
Ich verstehe den Artikel nicht.	*I don't understand the article.*
Die Lehrerin arbeitet morgen.	*The teacher is working tomorrow.*
Jeder Student hat ein Heft.	*Every student has a notebook.*
Sie wohnen in Berlin.	*They live in Berlin.*

■ In German, other elements such as accusative nouns and adverbs of time and place can precede the verb. When they do, the subject is moved to a position after the verb to preserve the verb as second element of the sentence.

Heute schwimmen wir.	*We're (going) swimming today.*
Den Artikel verstehe ich nicht.	*I don't understand the article.*
Morgen arbeitet die Lehrerin.	*The teacher is working tomorrow.*
Ein Heft hat jeder Student.	*Every student has a notebook.*
In Berlin wohnen sie.	*They live in Berlin.*

■ The element placed first shows the topic of the sentence, that is, the person or thing you are talking about. The element in first position does not give new information.

„Was tut ihr heute?"	*"What are you doing today?"*
„Heute schwimmen wir."	*"We're going swimming today."*
vs.	
„Wann schwimmt ihr?"	*"When are you going swimming?"*
„Wir schwimmen heute."	*"We're going swimming today."*

Vokabular

bleiben *to remain*	**morgen** *tomorrow*
bis *until*	**oft** *often*
das *that*	**sagen** *to say*
gehen *to go*	**später** *later*
das Heft *notebook*	**studieren** *to study*
jetzt *now*	**übermorgen** *day after tomorrow*
kommen *to come*	**die Übung** *exercise, practice* (pl. **die Übungen**)
der Kuli *ballpoint pen*	**verreist** *gone away, away on a trip*
der Monat *month*	**die Woche** *week*

Temporalausdrücke (Expressions of time)

die ganze Woche *all week, the entire week*

den ganzen Monat *all month, the entire month*

den ganzen Tag *all day long*

jeden Monat *every month*

jeden Tag *every day*

jede Woche *every week*

Die Wochentage (Days of the week)

All days of the week are masculine in German.

der Montag *Monday;* **am Montag** *on Monday;* **montags** *on Mondays*

der Dienstag *Tuesday;* **am Dienstag** *on Tuesday;* **dienstags**
on Tuesdays

der Mittwoch *Wednesday;* **am Mittwoch** *on Wednesday;* **mittwochs**
on Wednesdays

der Donnerstag *Thursday;* **am Donnerstag** *on Thursday;*
donnerstags *on Thursdays*

der Freitag *Friday;* **am Freitag** *on Friday;* **freitags** *on Fridays*

der Samstag *Saturday;* **am Samstag** *on Saturday;* **samstags**
on Saturdays
or
der Sonnabend *Saturday;* **am Sonnabend** *on Saturday;* **sonnabends**
on Saturdays

der Sonntag *Sunday;* **am Sonntag** *on Sunday;* **sonntags** *on Sundays*

A. Wortstellung. *(Word order.)* Rewrite the following sentences moving the element in italics to first position and changing the word order accordingly. Remember that the verb must be the second element in the sentence.

Beispiel Wir arbeiten *am Freitag* nicht.
➤ Am Freitag arbeiten wir nicht.

1. Großvater wartet *dort drüben.*

   _____

2. Wir bleiben *sonntags* zu Hause.

   _____

3. Ich schwimme *morgen.*

   _____

4. Du glaubst *das* nicht.

   _____

5. Die Kinder essen gern *Eis.*

   _____

6. Ich suche *den Kuli.*

   _____

7. Er kommt *am Montag.*

   _____

8. Helga ist *jetzt* verreist.

   _____

B. Nein. Answer each of the following questions about when people are doing things in the negative. Put the time word or phrase in first position in your answers. Replace noun subjects with pronouns.

Beispiel Fährt Hans morgen?
➤ Nein, morgen fährt er nicht.

1. Liest du jetzt?

   _____

2. Spielen die Studenten dienstags Fußball?

_____

3. Arbeitet Herr Müller heute?

_____

4. Ist das Kaufhaus morgen offen?

_____

5. Studiert Johann jeden Tag Deutsch?

_____

6. Trinkt Frau Dreyer jeden Tag Kaffee?

_____

7. Haben wir heute Biologie?

_____

8. Bleibt ihr bis Mittwoch hier?

_____

Sport (Sports)

Germany offers its citizens and tourists the enjoyment of winter and summer sports. There is skiing in the German Alps in the south, and swimming at the beaches of the North and Baltic seas in the north and in many lakes throughout the country. Germans love to be out in nature, and hiking through the German countryside is a favorite pastime for people of all ages. Germans are great sports fans too. Soccer is the most popular sport in Germany, and the excellent German national team has won the World Cup three times. Tennis has become a very popular sport, especially since the celebrated German champions Boris Becker and Steffi Graf have gained international acclaim by winning all the major tennis tournaments. At the age of 18, Becker was the youngest person ever to win the Wimbledon title.

C. Gespräch. *(Conversation.)* Answer each question in the negative, placing the element being asked about in initial position. Then tell what is true, following normal word order. Replace noun subjects with pronouns in your answers.

Beispiel Studiert Karl Deutsch? / Spanisch
➤ Nein, Deutsch studiert er nicht. Er studiert Spanisch.

1. Kommt Ulrike morgen? / am Donnerstag

   _____

2. Hast du das Heft? / das Buch

   _____

3. Warten die Kinder hier? / dort drüben

   _____

4. Arbeitet dein Vater in Berlin? / in Wien

   _____

5. Spielen die Studenten Schach? / Fußball

   _____

6. Wohnt ihr hier in der Nähe? / weit weg

   _____

7. Öffnet Klaus die Tür? / das Fenster

   _____

8. Besuchen die Touristen das Museum? / das Rathaus

   _____

D. Was gibt es zum Abendessen? *(What's for dinner?)* Say that you don't like the food being served for dinner.

Beispiel Wurst
> ➤ Zum Abendessen gibt es Wurst. Schade! Wurst esse ich nicht gern.

Das Abendessen (Dinner)

das Apfelmuß *applesauce*	**die Kartoffeln** *potatoes*
der Fisch *fish*	**der Reis** *rice*
das Fleisch *meat*	**das Rindfleisch** *beef*
das Hähnchen *chicken*	**der Schinken** *ham*
das Kalbfleisch *veal*	

---

1. Reis

2. Hähnchen

3. Schinken

4. Kartoffeln

5. Apfelmuß

6. Kalbfleisch

7. Fisch

8. Rindfleisch

II. Yes/No Questions

■ To ask a question in German that expects the answer of either yes or no, you put the subject after the verb. Yes/No questions are therefore sentences in which the verb is in first position.

Ist der Lehrer hier?	*Is the teacher here?*
Angelt Johann gern?	*Does Johann like to fish?*
Arbeitet ihr heute?	*Are you working today?*
Brauchst du einen Kuli?	*Do you need a pen?*

Remember that yes/no questions can also be formed by adding **nicht wahr** at the end of the question.

Sie kommen morgen, nicht wahr?	*They're coming tomorrow, aren't they?*

E. Die neue Schule. You're new at school. Ask one of the students you've become friendly with about what things are like at school.

Beispiel   die Studenten / sein / nett
➤ Sind die Studenten nett?

1. die Studenten / sein / fleißig

   _____

2. der Lehrer / sein / interessant

   _____

3. du / lesen / jeden Tag

   _____

4. du / tragen / jeden Tag / die Schultasche

   _____

5. wir / brauchen / einen Taschenrechner

   _____

6. ihr / spielen / Fußball

   _____

7. ihr / schreiben / jede Woche / einen Aufsatz

_____

8. haben / jeder Student / ein Heft

_____

F. Neue Freunde. *(New friends.)* Now you want to find out what the students at your new school like to do. Asks questions as in the model.

Beispiel   Liselotte / Schach spielen
      ➤ Spielt Liselotte gern Schach?

1. Hans und Fritz / angeln

_____

2. Ursula / studieren

_____

3. Birgit und Bernd / tanzen

_____

4. Max / rudern

_____

5. Rolf und Josef / Fußball spielen

_____

6. Silke / lesen

_____

7. du / zeichnen

_____

8. Ingrid und Meike / wandern

_____

G. Stadtbesuch. *(Visit to the city.)* Turn these statements into questions for your German friend who is showing you around her city.

Beispiel Das ist ein Kaufhaus.
> ➤ Ist das ein Kaufhaus?

In der Stadt (In the city)

bauen *to build*

bummeln *to stroll;* **einen Schaufensterbummel machen** *to go window-shopping*

die Fußgängerzone *pedestrian-only zone;* **in der Fußgängerzone** *in the pedestrian zone*

das Schloß *castle*

die U-Bahn *subway*

die Vororte (plural) *suburbs*

---

1. Das Büro ist heute offen.

   _____

2. Es gibt hier ein Schwimmbad.

   _____

3. Die Stadt baut eine U-Bahn.

   _____

4. Die Stadt hat einen Park.

   _____

5. Du bummelst oft in der Fußgängerzone.

   _____

6. Die Stadt hat ein Schloß.

   _____

7. Der Marktplatz ist hier in der Nähe.

   _____

8. Du fährst oft in die Vororte.

   _____

III. Use of *man*

■ German uses the pronoun **man** as an indefinite subject, similar to English *people, one,* or *you* and *they* when these pronouns are not specific. Often the English equivalent of **man** is in the passive voice, in other words, telling what was done rather than who did it. **Man** is always used with a third-person singular verb, the **er/sie/es** form.

Hier spricht man Deutsch.	*German is spoken here.*
Man ißt gut in Deutschland.	*One eats/People eat/You eat well in Germany.*
Wie sagt man «calculator» auf Deutsch?	*How do you say "calculator" in German?*
Man sagt «Taschenrechner».	*You say "Taschenrechner."*

H. Sprachen. *(Languages.)* Talk about the languages used here using **man** and the verb given in each case. Notice that in some sentences the name of the language is preceded by **auf**: **auf Deutsch** *(in German).*

Beispiel   gern haben / Deutsch
      ➤ Hier hat man gern Deutsch.

1. sprechen / Französisch

   _____

2. verstehen / Deutsch

   _____

3. studieren / Englisch

   _____

4. lesen / Italienisch

   _____

5. schreiben / Chinesisch

   _____

6. singen / auf Spanisch

   _____

7. plaudern / auf Russisch

   _____

8. arbeiten / auf Japanisch

   _____

I. Schulfragen. *(Questions about school.)* Use yes/no questions with **man** to find out about your new school.

Beispiel   Französisch und Deutsch lernen
➤ Lernt man Französisch und Deutsch?

Die Schule

bringen *to bring*	**das Mittagessen** *lunch*
die Hausaufgaben (plural) *homework*	**der Sport** *physical education*
lernen *to learn, study*	**viel** *a lot*

---

1. jeden Tag Hausaufgaben haben

   _____

2. viel lesen

   _____

3. jede Woche einen Aufsatz schreiben

   _____

4. Fußball spielen

   _____

5. jeden Tag einen Taschenrechner bringen

   _____

6. jeden Tag Sport haben

   _____

7. das Mittagessen kaufen

   _____

8. Schach spielen

   _____

Arbeitsheft: A Workbook for German Grammar and Communication

J. **Und du?** Answer the following questions in complete sentences.

1. Hast du jeden Tag Deutsch?

   _____

2. In deiner Schule spielt man oft Fußball?

   _____

3. Hast du lieber Deutsch oder Mathematik?

   _____

4. Bummelst du gern? Wo? In der Fußgängerzone?

   _____

5. Ißt du lieber Hähnchen oder Rindfleisch?

   _____

K. **Aufsatz.** Tell a new student from Germany about your school. Try to use as many sentences as possible with **man** as the subject. Write a paragraph of 5 to 6 sentences.

Plural of Nouns (Nominative and Accusative); Information Questions; Telling Time; Numbers 21–10,000

I. Plural of Nouns (Nominative and Accusative)

■ In the plural in German, all three genders have the same articles. The nominative and accusative plural article is **die** for all nouns. There are various ways to form the plural of nouns in German so you have to learn the plural along with the singular. Here are examples of different types of plurals.

Notes:

1. Some German nouns do not change in the plural. Most masculine nouns ending in -**er**, -**en**, or -**el** and neuter nouns ending in -**er**, -**en**, -**el**, -**chen**, and -**lein** do not change their form in the plural.

singular	plural
der Computer	die Computer *computers*
der Lehrer	die Lehrer *teachers*
der Onkel	die Onkel *uncles*
das Fenster	die Fenster *windows*
das Hähnchen	die Hähnchen *chickens*
das Zimmer	die Zimmer *rooms*

2. Most feminine nouns add -**n** to form the plural if the singular ends in -**e** or -**er**, or -**en** if the singular ends in a consonant. No feminine nouns are the same in both singular and plural.

■ Feminine nouns that add -**n** to form the plural:

singular	plural
die Blume	die Blumen *flowers*
die Briefmarke	die Briefmarken *stamps*
die Fußgängerzone	die Fußgängerzonen *pedestrian-only zones*
die Schule	die Schulen *schools*
die Schwester	die Schwestern *sisters*
die Woche	die Wochen *weeks*

■ Feminine nouns that add -**en** to form the plural:

singular	plural
die Bibliothek	die Bibliotheken *libraries*
die Frau	die Frauen *women*
die Übung	die Übungen *exercises*

- Feminine nouns ending in **-in** add **-nen** to form the plural:

  die Freundin   **die Freundinnen** *girlfriends*

3. Many masculine and neuter nouns form the plural by adding **-e.**

singular	plural
der Besuch	die Besuche *visits*
der Bleistift	die Bleistifte *pencils*
der Dom	die Dome *cathedrals*
der Hund	die Hunde *dogs*
der Leuchtstift	die Leuchtstifte *highlighters*
der Monat	die Monate *months*
der Tag	die Tage *days*
das Heft	die Hefte *notebooks*
das Jahr	die Jahre *years*

4. Many German nouns form the plural by adding an umlaut to the stressed vowel.

   - Some masculine nouns ending in **-en, -el, -er** and the feminine nouns **Mutter** and **Tochter** form their plural solely by adding an umlaut to the stressed vowel.

singular	plural
der Apfel	die Äpfel *apples*
der Bruder	die Brüder *brothers*
der Garten	die Gärten *gardens*
der Hafen	die Häfen *harbors*
der Vater	die Väter *fathers*
die Mutter	die Mütter *mothers*
die Tochter	die Töchter *daughters*

   - Many masculine nouns that form their plural by adding **-e** also add an umlaut to the stressed vowel.

singular	plural
der Bahnhof	die Bahnhöfe *railway stations*
der Marktplatz	die Marktplätze *marketplaces*
der Saft	die Säfte *juices*
der Schulhof	die Schulhöfe *schoolyards*
der Sohn	die Söhne *sons*

- Feminine nouns that have their plural in **-e** add an umlaut over the stressed vowel.

singular	plural
die Angst	die Ängste *fears*
die Stadt	die Städte *cities*
die Wurst	die Würste *sausages*

5. Some masculine and many neuter nouns form their plural by adding **-er** to the singular form. Many of these also add an umlaut.

singular	plural
der Mann	die Männer *men*
das Buch	die Bücher *books*
das Dorf	die Dörfer *villages*
das Haus	die Häuser *houses*
das Kaufhaus	die Kaufhäuser *department stores*
das Kind	die Kinder *children*

6. Words borrowed from foreign languages such as English and French often form their plural in **-s.**

singular	plural
das Baby	die Babys *babies*
der Bonbon	die Bonbons *candy*
das Hotel	die Hotels *hotels*
das Kino	die Kinos *movie theaters*
der Park	die Parks *parks*
das Restaurant	die Restaurants *restaurants*

7. Some nouns have irregular plurals.

singular	plural
der Hörsaal	die Hörsäle *lecture halls*
die Mensa	die Mensen *cafeterias*
das Museum	die Museen *museums*
das Stadion	die Stadien *stadiums*

A. Hier in der Stadt. Write conversations in which one student informs another that the city they are in has two of everything. Remember to use the accusative case after **es gibt.**

Beispiel Park
➤ Gibt es hier einen Park?
    Es gibt hier zwei Parks.

Vokabular

die Bank (pl. **die Banken**) *bank*   **das Kunstmuseum** *art museum*

der Busbahnhof *bus station*   **der Laden** (pl. **die Läden**) *store*

die Imbißstube *fast food stand*   **der Markt** (pl. **die Märkte**) *market*

---

1. Fußballstadion

   _____

   _____

2. Kunstmuseum

   _____

   _____

3. Busbahnhof

   _____

   _____

4. Imbißstube

   _____

   _____

5. Bank

   _____

   _____

➤➤➤➤➤

6. Markt

_____

_____

7. Bibliothek

_____

_____

8. Dom

_____

_____

9. Hotel

_____

_____

10. Fußgängerzone

_____

_____

B. Im Plural. Rewrite each of the following sentences by changing all the nouns to the plural. Make all other necessary changes.

Beispiel Das Dorf hat eine Bank.
➤ Die Dörfer haben Banken.

1. Das Kind hat ein Heft.

_____

2. Die Studentin hat den Lehrer gern.

_____

3. Die Frau und der Mann suchen das Kaufhaus.

_____

4. Das Hotel hat ein Restaurant.

   _____

5. Die Universität hat einen Hörsaal.

   _____

6. Der Student hat die Imbißstube gern.

   _____

7. Der Sohn und die Tochter haben ein Auto.

   _____

8. Die Lehrerin braucht einen Bleistift und einen Leuchtstift.

   _____

C. **Im Plural.** Given what you have learned about forming plurals in German, can you write the plurals of the following nouns? Remember that compound nouns usually form their plural by pluralizing the last noun in the compound (e.g., **Kunstmuseum** > **Kunstmuseen**).

1. die Brücke   _____

2. der Großvater   _____

3. die Tante   _____

4. der Drucker   _____

5. der Flughafen   _____

6. die Großmutter   _____

7. die Pizza   _____

8. die Straße   _____

Shopping

- German cities traditionally have main shopping streets in the downtown area and in certain neighborhoods. There are department stores and smaller shops, as well as cafés and **Buden** or **Imbißstuben** (*fast food stands*). The main shopping area in Berlin is the **Kurfürstendamm,** in Frankfurt it's the **Zeil,** in Munich the **Maximilianstraße,** and in Düsseldorf the **Königsallee.** In shopping for food, there are supermarkets as well as the traditional specialized shops. German stores offer a great variety of foods, due in part to the large influx of foreigners. This variety is particularly in evidence at the large central markets, such as Frankfurt's **Kleinmarkthalle,** Hamburg's **Fischermarkt** or **Käsemarkt,** and Munich's **Viktualienmarkt.**
- The **Flohmarkt** (*flea market*), an outdoor flea market operating on weekends, is a popular feature of German culture. One can purchase almost any used or new item at the **Flohmarkt.**
- American-style shopping malls are becoming more popular in Germany, as they are throughout the world. Inner-city shopping districts are mostly located in pedestrian-only zones.

II. Information Questions

- Information questions begin with a question word such as *what?*, *when?*, *who?* In German, the question word comes first in the sentence so the subject must follow the verb. The most common question words in German are:

Was? *What?*	**Wessen?** *Whose?*
Wer? *Who?*	**Wo?** *Where?*
Wen? *Whom?*	**Wie?** *How?*
Warum? *Why?*	**Wann?** *When?*

Notes:

1. German distinguishes between **wo?** which asks about *location* and **wohin?** which is used with verbs of motion and asks about *direction*.

Wo ist der Busbahnhof?	*Where is the bus station?*
Wohin fährt der Bus?	*Where is the bus going?*

2. **Wieviel?** means *how much?* and is used before singular nouns. **Wie viele?** means *how many?* and is used before plural nouns.

Wieviel Milch trinkt das Kind?	*How much milk does the child drink?*
Wie viele Hefte brauchst du?	*How many notebooks do you need?*

3. *What kind of?* is **was für ein?** before singular nouns and **was für?** before plural nouns. The **ein** changes for gender and case in the singular.

Was für ein Laden ist das?	*What kind of store is this?*
Was für einen Computer hast du?	*What kind of computer do you have?*
Was für eine Wurst ißt du?	*What kind of sausage are you eating?*
Was für Kleider trägst du gern?	*What kind of clothing do you like to wear?*

D. Das Fragewort fehlt. *(The question word is missing.)* Add the missing question words that would be logical in these exchanges.

Beispiel   __Wer__ arbeitet hier?
(Herr Müller)

1. _____ wohnen Susi und Bärbel?
(In Berlin)

2. _____ Bücher hast du heute?
(Drei)

3. _____ trinkt Johann?
(Eine Limonade)

4. _____ fährt der Autobus?
(Nach Berlin)

5. _____ Haus ist das?
(Das Haus von Frau Breitsprecher)

6. _____ siehst du dort drüben?
(Dieter)

7. _____ bleibst du zu Hause?
(Ich bin müde)

8. _____ fahren Sie nach Wien?
(Übermorgen)

E. Wie ist die Frage? Write the question that would have elicited each of the following responses. The question word should refer to the element in italics in the response.

Beispiel ➢ <u>Was ist das?</u>
Das ist *ein Drucker.*

1. _____

    Das ist *der Lehrer.*

2. _____

    Die Studenten kommen *morgen.*

3. _____

    Helga sitzt *dort drüben.*

4. _____

    Sie studiert *fleißig.*

5. _____

    Wir fahren *nach Zürich.*

6. _____

    Es ist *halb fünf.*

7. _____

    Ich habe *einen neuen* Computer.

8. _____

    Der Film beginnt um *drei Uhr zehn.*

9. _____

    Moritz besucht *Karl.*

10. _____

    Wir haben *drei* Disketten.

III. Telling Time; Numbers 21–10,000

- To ask the time in German, you say „Wieviel Uhr ist es?" or „Wie spät ist es?" To ask at what time something is happening, use the phrase „Um wieviel Uhr?" Here is how you tell time in German.

Es ist ein Uhr.	*It is one o'clock.*
Es ist zwei Uhr.	*It is two o'clock.*
Es ist Viertel nach zwei.	*It is a quarter after two.*
Es ist zwei Uhr fünfzehn.	*It is two-fifteen.*
Es ist halb drei.	*It is half past two.*
Es ist zwei Uhr dreißig.	*It is two-thirty.*
Es ist Viertel vor drei.	*It is a quarter to three.*
Es ist zwei Uhr fünfundvierzig.	*It is two forty-five.*
Gegen drei Uhr.	*About three o'clock.*

Die Uhr

die Minute *minute* (pl. die Minuten)

die Sekunde *second* (pl. die Sekunden)

die Stunde *hour, class period* (pl. die Stunden)

- Numbers 21–10,000

21	einundzwanzig	100	einhundert, hundert
22	zweiundzwanzig	146	hundertsechsundvierzig
23	dreiundzwanzig	200	zweihundert
24	vierundzwanzig	300	dreihundert
25	fünfundzwanzig	400	vierhundert
26	sechsundzwanzig	500	fünfhundert
27	siebenundzwanzig	600	sechshundert
28	achtundzwanzig	700	siebenhundert
29	neunundzwanzig	800	achthundert
30	dreißig	900	neunhundert
31	einunddreißig	1000	eintausend, tausend
40	vierzig	1100	tausendeinhundert OR elfhundert
50	fünfzig	1283	tausendzweihundertdreiundachtzig
60	sechzig		OR zwölfhundertdreiundachtzig
70	siebzig	2000	zweitausend
80	achtzig	2359	zweitausenddreihundertneunundfünfzig
90	neunzig	10,000	zehntausend

Remember that German usually expresses the years with **hundert** up to two thousand:

1492 vierzehnhundertzweiundneunzig

F. Die Uhr. Answer the question „**Wie spät ist es?**" according to the timepieces below.

1. _____

2. _____

3. _____

4. _____

5. _____

6. _____

Arbeitsheft: A Workbook for German Grammar and Communication

G. Jahre. Write out the following years.

1. 1056 _____

2. 1230 _____

3. 1348 _____

4. 1453 _____

5. 1536 _____

6. 1620 _____

7. 1776 _____

8. 1865 _____

9. 1999 _____

10. 2001 _____

H. Und du? Answer the following questions in complete sentences.

1. Um wieviel Uhr beginnt die Deutschstunde?

2. Wie viele Studenten studieren Deutsch?

3. Wie heißt der Lehrer (die Lehrerin)?

4. Wie viele Bleistifte, Hefte, und Bücher hast du?

5. Wie alt bist du?

I. Aufsatz. Describe one of your classes. Tell what time class begins and ends, what the teacher's name is, how many students there are, what kind of homework you do, and at what time you do it.

Dative Case; Weak Masculine Nouns;
Other Uses of the Dative; Some Constructions
*with **mit** and **bei**; The Verb **gefallen***

I. The Dative Case

- The dative case labels the indirect object, the person to whom or for whom something is done. The dative is shown by the form of the article. Masculine and neuter nouns use the definite article **dem** in the dative singular. Feminine nouns use the definite article **der.**

  The dative indefinite article is **einem** for masculine and neuter nouns, **einer** for feminine nouns in the singular form.

  In the plural, the dative definite article is **den** before all nouns. An **-n** is added to the plural form unless the plural ends in **-n** or **-s.**

  den Kindern *to/for the children*

  den Babys *to/for the babies*

- The following verbs often appear with a noun or pronoun in the dative referring to a person as well as with a noun in the accusative referring to a thing:

bringen *to bring*	**schenken** *to give as a gift*
empfehlen *to recommend*	**schicken** *to send*
erzählen *to tell, recount*	**schreiben** *to write*
geben *to give*	**schulden** *to owe*
leihen *to lend*	**verkaufen** *to sell*
reichen *to pass (at the table); to hand*	**zeigen** *to show*
sagen *to say*	

Ich zeige dem Lehrer die Hausaufgaben.	*I show the teacher the homework.*
Der Mann schickt der Frau einen Blumenstrauß.	*The man sends the woman a bouquet.*

- The dative pronouns are:

mir *to/for me*	**uns** *to/for us*
dir *to/for you*	**euch** *to/for you*
ihm *to/for him*	**ihnen** *to/for them*
ihr *to/for her*	**Ihnen** *to/for you* (formal)

- **Wem** is the dative question word.

Wem erzählt ihr die Geschichte? Den Kindern?	*Whom are you telling the story to? The children?*
Ja, wir erzählen ihnen die Geschichte.	*Yes, we are telling them the story.*
Was reichst du der Lehrerin?	*What are you handing the teacher?*
Ich gebe ihr den Aufsatz.	*I'm giving her the composition.*

A. Gute Freundinnen. Gisela and Hannelore are always willing to help their friends. Write out what they will do in each case using the verb in parentheses and an appropriate indirect object pronoun.

Beispiel   Hans hat keinen Bleistift. (einen Bleistift geben)
   ➤ Wir geben ihm einen Bleistift.

Dinge (Things)

der Brief *letter* (pl. **die Briefe**)

der Geburtstag *birthday* (pl. **die Geburtstage**)

die Fotografie *photo* (pl. **die Fotografien**)

der Stadtbummel *walk through town* (pl. **die Stadtbummel**)

die Wohnung *apartment* (pl. **die Wohnungen**)

der Reisepaß *passport* (pl. **die Reisepässe**)

das Salz *salt*

die Suppe *soup*

der Zucker *sugar*

---

1. Manfred liest kein Buch. (ein Buch empfehlen)

    _____

2. Christoph hat morgen Geburtstag. (ein Hemd schenken)

    _____

3. Sabina und Britta wissen nicht, wo das Büro ist. (die Adresse sagen)

    _____

4. Markus und ich haben keine Wohnung. (eine Wohnung finden)

    _____

➤➤➤➤➤

5. Oma trinkt gern Tee mit Zucker. (den Zucker reichen)

   _____

6. Ich habe keinen Computer. (einen alten Computer verkaufen)

   _____

7. Gustav braucht hundert Mark. (hundert Mark schicken)

   _____

8. Anneliese hat kein Brot. (Brot bringen)

   _____

II. Weak Masculine Nouns

■ Some masculine nouns add -en in all cases except the nominative singular. Study the forms of **der Mensch** (*person*).

	singular	plural
nominative	der Mensch	die Menschen
dative	dem Menschen	den Menschen
accusative	den Menschen	die Menschen

A few of these nouns add -n. Study the forms of **der Junge** (*boy*).

	singular	plural
nominative	der Junge	die Jungen
dative	dem Jungen	den Jungen
accusative	den Jungen	die Jungen

Some nouns that you are familiar with that are declined this way:

der Nachbar; dem/den Nachbarn (dem/den Nachbar is also possible)

der Student; dem/den Studenten

Note also **der Name** (*name*) (**dem/den Namen;** pl. **die Namen**) and masculine nouns of profession ending in -**ist** have the ending -**en** in the dative and accusative.

B. In der Berufswelt. *(In the working world.)* Complete the following sentences with the correct form of the article and noun in parentheses.

1. (die Polizistin)   Wir zeigen _____ die Reisepässe.

2. (der Geschäftsmann)   Die Bank leiht _____ Geld.

3. (die Rechtsanwälte)   Ich erzähle _____ die ganze Geschichte.

4. (der Programmierer) Sie verkaufen _____ einen
neuen Computer.

5. (die Ingenieure) Wir zeigen _____ das
Projekt.

6. (der Verkäufer) Du sagst _____, was du
brauchst.

7. (die Architektin) Ihr zeigt _____ die
Wohnung.

8. (der Zahnarzt) Wir schulden _____ viel
Geld.

Berufe (Professions)

Note that feminine nouns ending in **-in** form the plural by adding
-nen.

der Arbeiter (pl. **die Arbeiter**)/**die Arbeiterin** *worker*

der Architekt (pl. **die Architekten**)/**die Architektin** *architect*
(note: **dem/den Architekten**)

der Arzt (pl. **die Ärzte**)/**die Ärztin** *doctor*

der Bäcker (pl. **die Bäcker**)/**die Bäckerin** *baker*

der Chemiker (pl. **die Chemiker**)/**die Chemikerin** *chemist*

der Gärtner (pl. **die Gärtner**)/**die Gärtnerin** *gardener*

die Geschäftsfrau *businesswoman* (pl. **die Geschäftsfrauen**)

der Geschäftsmann *businessman* (pl. **die Geschäftsleute**)

der Ingenieur (pl. **die Ingenieure**)/**die Ingenieurin** *engineer*

der Krankenpfleger *male nurse* (pl. **die Krankenpfleger**)

die Krankenschwester *female nurse* (pl. **die Krankenschwestern**)

der Metzger (pl. **die Metzger**)/**die Metzgerin** *butcher*

der Polizist (pl. **die Polizisten**)/**die Polizistin** *policeman/
policewoman*

der Programmierer (pl. **die Programmierer**)/**die Programmiererin**
programmer

der Rechtsanwalt (pl. **die Rechtsanwälte**)/**die Rechtsanwältin**
lawyer

der Verkäufer (pl. **die Verkäufer**)/**die Verkäuferin** *salesman/
saleswoman*

der Zahnarzt (pl. **die Zahnärzte**)/**die Zahnärztin** *dentist*

III. Other Uses of the Dative

■ The dative in German is used after the following verbs:

antworten *to answer*	**gratulieren (zum Geburtstag)** *to congratulate someone (on the occasion of their birthday)*
folgen *to follow*	
gehorchen *to obey*	**helfen** (e > i) *to help*
gehören *to belong to*	**schaden** *to harm*

■ The dative is always used after the following prepositions:

aus *out of, from*	**seit** *since*
bei *by, at, at the house of*	**von** *from, of*
mit *with*	**zu** *to*
nach *to, toward*	

The dative is used after the following prepositions when they express location (as opposed to direction):

auf *on*	**über** *over, above*
an *at*	**unter** *under*
in *in*	**zwischen** *between*
neben *next to*	

Some of the above prepositions contract with the dative form of the masculine and neuter article:

an + dem > am

bei + dem > beim

in + dem > im

von + dem > vom

zu + dem > zum

The preposition zu also contracts with the dative form of the feminine article:

zu + der > zur

C. Was fehlt? *(What's missing?)* Complete the following sentences with the correct form of the article and noun in parentheses.

1. (die Freunde) Ich gratuliere _____ zum Geburtstag.

2. (der Lehrer) Die Studenten schenken _____ ein Buch.

3. (der Polizist) Wir folgen _____ .

4. (die Ärzte)   Die Krankenschwester helfen _____.

5. (die Ingenieurin)   Wir zeigen _____ das Projekt.

6. (die Verkäuferin)   Du sagst _____, was du brauchst.

7. (der Architekt)   Ihr zeigt _____ die Wohnung.

8. (die Zahnärztin)   Wir schulden _____ viel Geld.

D. Deshalb. *(Therefore.)* Use the words in parentheses, a dative form, and the word **deshalb** (*therefore*) to explain what people are doing in each of the following situations.

Beispiel   Johann hat morgen Geburtstag. (du / ein Buch kaufen)
➢ Deshalb kaufst du ihm ein Buch.

1. Die Kinder hören Geschichten gern. (wir / lesen eine Geschichte vor)

   _____

2. Die Architektin sieht gern Fotografien. (ich / meine Fotografien zeigen)

   _____

3. Opa braucht Salz für die Suppe. (ich / das Salz reichen)

   _____

4. Wir haben kein Auto. (du / ein Auto leihen)

   _____

5. Die Arbeiter haben Durst. (wir / Limonade bringen)

   _____

6. Gisela schreibt mir oft. (ich / einen Brief schreiben)

   _____

7. Ihr wißt nicht, wo Magda wohnt. (wir / die Adresse sagen)

   _____

8. Die Babys haben Durst. (die Mütter / Milch geben)

   _____

E. Wo arbeiten Sie? *(Where do you work?)* Answer these questions with the preposition **in** and the noun in parentheses preceded by the indefinite article.

Beispiel   Wo arbeitet der Lehrer? (Schule)
    ➤ Er arbeitet in einer Schule.

Orte (Places)

die Baustelle *construction site* (pl. **die Baustellen**)

der Betrieb *company, factory* (pl. **die Betriebe**)

der Garten *garden* (pl. **die Gärten**)

die Jugendherberge *youth hostel* (pl. **die Jugendherbergen**)

das Krankenhaus *hospital* (pl. **die Krankenhäuser**)

die Stadtmitte *center of town, downtown* (pl. **die Stadtmitten**)

der Strand *beach* (pl. **die Strände**)

der Supermarkt *supermarket* (pl. **die Supermärkte**)

---

1. Wo arbeitet der Krankenpfleger? (Krankenhaus)

   _____

2. Wo arbeiten die Rechtsanwälte? (Büro)

   _____

3. Wo arbeitet der Verkäufer? (Kaufhaus)

   _____

4. Wo arbeitet die Polizistin? (Bank)

   _____

5. Wo arbeiten die Arbeiter? (Baustelle)

   _____

6. Wo arbeitet die Chemikerin? (Labor)

   _____

7. Wo arbeitet der Gärtner? (Garten)

_____

8. Wo arbeitet die Ingenieurin? (Betrieb)

_____

F. Wo? Answer the following questions about location using the prepositions and nouns in parentheses. Use contractions of the prepositions with the definite articles where possible.

Beispiel Wo sitzt Oma? (in / Garten)
       ➤ Sie sitzt im Garten.

1. Wo sind die Touristen? (an / Bahnhof)

_____

2. Wo wohnen die Studenten? (in / Jugendherberge)

_____

3. Wo spielen die Kinder? (an / Strand)

_____

4. Wo kaufst du Fleisch? (in / Supermarkt)

_____

5. Wo schläft der Hund? (unter / Tisch)

_____

6. Wo sind Hans und Jutta? (in / Kino)

_____

7. Wo ist der Polizist? (auf / Straße)

_____

8. Wo studiert ihr? (in / Bibliothek)

_____

G. Wohin geht man? Tell where the following people are going, using the places in parentheses and the phrases **gehen zu/fahren zu.** Use contractions of **zu** + definite article where possible.

Beispiel   Wohin gehen Hedda und Jürgen? (Jugendherberge)
➤ Sie gehen zur Jugendherberge.

1. Wohin fährt der Autobus Nummer 2? (Bibliothek)

_____

2. Wohin geht ihr? (Stadtmitte)

_____

3. Wohin fährst du? (Bahnhof)

_____

4. Wohin geht Martin? (Arzt)

_____

5. Wohin fährt Lise? (Flughafen)

_____

6. Wohin gehen die Jungen? (Zahnärzte)

_____

7. Wohin geht der Arbeiter? (Baustelle)

_____

8. Wohin gehen die Nachbarn? (Rechtsanwälte)

_____

IV. Some Constructions with *mit* and *bei*

■ The preposition **mit** is used to express a means of transportation.

Wir fahren mit dem Autobus.   *We're going by bus.*

■ The preposition **bei** often means *at the house of* or *in the shop of.*

Wir essen beim Nachbar.   *We are eating at our neighbor's.*
Mutter ist beim Bäcker.   *Mother is at the baker's.*

H. Man fährt. Tell how the following people are traveling.

Beispiel   Helmut / Bus
> Helmut fährt mit dem Bus.

Verkehrsmittel (Transportation)

das Auto *car* (pl. **die Autos**)

der Bus *bus* (pl. **die Busse**)

das Fahrrad *bicycle* (pl. **die Fahrräder**)

das Flugzeug *airplane* (pl. **die Flugzeuge**)

die S-Bahn *suburban railway* (pl. **die S-Bahnen**)

das Schiff *ship* (pl. **die Schiffe**)

der Schnellzug *express train* (pl. **die Schnellzüge**)

die Straßenbahn *streetcar* (pl. **die Straßenbahnen**)

die U-Bahn *subway* (pl. **die U-Bahnen**)

der Zug *train* (pl. **die Züge**)

---

1. Gisela / S-Bahn

   _____

2. ich / Auto

   _____

3. meine Freunde / Schnellzug

   _____

4. die Touristen / Flugzeug

   _____

5. die Arbeiter / Straßenbahn

   _____

6. meine Familie / Zug

   _____

7. Hannelore / Schiff

   _____

8. wir / U-Bahn

   _____

Verkehrsmittel

- Germany has an excellent transportation system that makes it easy to get around the country. Buses join cities, towns, and urban centers, and the larger cities have extensive subway systems, known as the **U-Bahn.** The **S-Bahn,** or suburban trains, are high-speed lines that link larger towns and their suburbs. Streetcars are also a means of transport in some cities.
- The federal railway system, the **Bundesbahn,** provides very good service and is a popular way to travel. There are different types of trains, such as the **D-Zug** (the **Durchgangszug,** or through train); the **E-Zug** (the **Eilzug,** or fast train); and the **ICE** (or Intercity Express). The **ICE** is a high-speed train with fully equipped offices and other amenities.
- Many Germans and tourists get around by bicycle. Germany has a network of bicycle trails, and cities and towns usually have designated lanes for bicycles. German Rail's **Fahrrad am Bahnhof** (Bicycles at the Station) program allows people to rent bicycles at hundreds of train stations throughout the country.
- Germans also car-pool a lot, especially in urban centers, but also in provincial areas. There are **Mitfahrzentralen** in many cities, where you can call in ahead of time and reserve a ride. In contrast to earlier days, a speed limit is now imposed for most of the **Autobahn.** The limit varies from place to place. And, whereas many vacation-bound Germans used to take their cars, thus creating massive traffic jams (and frequent fatal accidents and pile-ups), a majority now choose to travel by train, arriving at their vacation spot more quickly and safely—and relaxed.
- Frankfurt International Airport, the hub of German air travel, is the second largest airport in Europe. Hamburg, Munich, and Düsseldorf also handle heavy international traffic.

V. The Verb *gefallen*

- The verb **gefallen** means *to like something*. With **gefallen,** the thing liked becomes the subject of the sentence. The person who likes the thing appears in the dative. **Gefallen** is used in the third-person singular (**gefällt**) or plural (**gefallen**).

Wie gefällt dir die Stadt?	*How do you like the city?*
Sie gefällt mir gut.	*I like it very much.*
Wie gefallen euch die Restaurants?	*How do you like the restaurants?*
Sie gefallen uns nicht.	*We don't like them.*

- **Es** can be used as the subject in questions and statements about liking places.

Gefällt es Ihnen in Berlin?	*Do you like it in Berlin?*
Ja, es gefällt mir gut hier.	*Yes, I like it here.*

I. **Stadtbummel.** A guide is taking a group of tourists around München (Munich), a famous German city in Bavaria. He asks individuals and groups how they like what they see. Write their answers.

Beispiel Wie gefällt Ihnen der Stadtbummel, Herr Schmidt?
> Er gefällt mir gut.

1. Wie gefallen euch die Parks, Kinder?

_____

2. Wie gefällt Ihnen das Kunstmuseum, Frau Müller?

_____

3. Wie gefällt Ihnen die Stadtmitte, meine Damen und Herren?

_____

4. Wie gefällt Ihnen die Fußgängerzone, Herr Becker?

_____

5. Wie gefallen Ihnen die Kaufhäuser, meine Damen und Herren?

_____

6. Wie gefällt Ihnen das Rathaus, Frau Bergmann?

_____

7. Wie gefallen euch die Restaurants, Kinder?

_____

8. Wie gefällt Ihnen das Hotel, meine Damen und Herren?

_____

J. **Nicht zufrieden.** Tell why each of these working people is dissatisfied. Use **nicht gefallen.** Place the person first in the sentence and remember to use the dative with the person.

Beispiel der Architekt / das Gebäude
> Dem Architekt gefällt das Gebäude nicht.

1. die Krankenschwester / das Krankenhaus

_____

2. die Rechtsanwälte / das Büro

_____

3. der Arbeiter / die Baustelle

_____

4. die Geschäftsfrauen / die Bank

_____

5. der Lehrer / die Schulen

_____

6. die Chemikerinnen / das Labor

_____

7. der Polizist / die Stadt

_____

8. die Ingenieure / die Betriebe

_____

K. Und du? Answer the following questions in complete sentences.

1. Wie gefällt dir die Schule? Wie gefallen dir die Lehrer?

_____

2. Gefällt dir die Stadt, wo du wohnst? Was gefällt dir (nicht)?

_____

3. Wie fährst du zur Schule?

_____

4. Fährst du oft mit dem Zug? Mit dem Bus?

_____

5. Dein Freund (Deine Freundin) hat Geburtstag. Was schenkst du ihm (ihr)?

_____

L. Aufsatz. Talk about how your friends and you help each other. What do you give or lend each other? What gifts do you exchange? Write a paragraph of five or six sentences, using the dative as many times as possible.

Demonstrative Adjectives; Possessive Adjectives; Accusative Form of Pronouns; Genitive (Possessive -s)

I. Demonstrative Adjectives

■ The demonstrative adjective **dieser** *this/that* (plural *these/those*) has the same endings as the definite article.

	masculine	feminine	neuter
nominative	dieser Mann	diese Frau	dieses Kind
dative	diesem Mann	dieser Frau	diesem Kind
accusative	diesen Mann	diese Frau	dieses Kind

In the plural, the demonstratives have the same forms for all three genders.

	masculine	feminine	neuter
nominative	diese Männer	diese Frauen	diese Kinder
dative	diesen Männer<u>n</u>	diesen Frauen	diesen Kinder<u>n</u>
accusative	diese Männer	diese Frauen	diese Kinder

The demonstrative **dieser** means both *this* and *that*.

Ich kaufe Gemüse in diesem Laden.	*I buy vegetables in this/that store.*
Diese Architektin hat ein Büro.	*This/That architect has an office.*

The definite article in German can also serve as a demonstrative. When it does, the article is stressed in speech. The definite article used as a demonstrative can mean either this or that (in the plural, either these or those).

Ich habe das Restaurant nicht gern.	*I don't like this/that restaurant.*
Deshalb esse ich nicht in dem Restaurant.	*That's why I don't eat at this/that restaurant.*
Diese Wohnungen sind modern.	*These/Those apartments are modern.*

A. Diese Dinge sind gut. A friend is looking for various items for school. You tell him or her which is good using **dieser** + noun.

Beispiel   Ich brauche ein Heft.
➤ Dieses Heft ist gut.

1. Ich brauche einen Bleistift.

_____

2. Ich brauche Disketten.

_____

3. Ich brauche einen Radiergummi.

_____

4. Ich brauche eine Schultasche.

_____

5. Ich brauche Leuchtstifte.

_____

6. Ich brauche einen Taschenrechner.

_____

7. Ich brauche ein Lineal.

_____

8. Ich brauche einen Block.

_____

B. In der Berufswelt. *(In the professional world.)* Create sentences from each string of elements adding the proper form of **dieser** before each noun referring to a profession or line of work.

Beispiel   Magda / arbeiten bei / Bäcker
➤ Magda arbeitet bei diesem Bäcker.

1. Johann / sprechen mit / Rechtsanwalt

_____

2. wir / arbeiten neben dem Büro von / Geschäftsfrau

_____

3. die Kinder / gehen zu / Ärzte

_____

4. die Studenten / warten in dem Büro von / Lehrer

_____

5. Ursula / schicken die Fotografien zu / Architekten

_____

6. meine Mutter / kaufen bei / Metzger

_____

7. die Touristen / sprechen mit / Polizisten

_____

8. mein Vater / arbeiten im Büro von / Ingenieure

_____

II. Possessive Adjectives

- Possessive adjectives in German agree with the noun they refer to in gender and case. Unlike **dieser,** which has the endings of the definite article, possessive adjectives have the endings of the indefinite article. This means that the possessives have no ending in the masculine nominative singular (**mein Freund**) or in the neuter nominative and neuter accusative singular (**mein Haus**). In all other forms, they have the same endings as **dieser.** Here are the possessive adjectives in German with the subject pronouns to which they correspond:

ich	mein _my_		wir	unser _our_
du	dein _your_		ihr	euer _your_
er, es	sein _his, its_		sie	ihr _their_
sie	ihr _her_		Sie	Ihr _your_ (formal)

singular

	masculine	feminine	neuter
nominative	mein Freund	meine Katze	mein Haus
dative	meinem Freund	meiner Katze	meinem Haus
accusative	meinen Freund	meine Katze	mein Haus

plural

nominative	meine Freunde, Katzen, Häuser
dative	meinen Freunden, Katzen, Häusern
accusative	meine Freunde, Katzen, Häuser

Unser and **euer** often drop the **e** before the final **r** before an ending beginning with **e.** The forms that drop the **e** are especially common in speech, but are used in writing as well.

singular

	masculine	feminine	neuter
nominative	unser Freund	unsre Katze	unser Haus
dative	unsrem Freund	unsrer Katze	unsrem Haus
accusative	unsren Freund	unsre Katze	unser Haus

	plural
nominative	unsre Freunde, Katzen, Häuser
dative	unsren Freunden, Katzen, Häusern
accusative	unsre Freunde, Katzen, Häuser

	singular		
	masculine	**feminine**	**neuter**
nominative	euer Freund	eure Katze	euer Haus
dative	eurem Freund	eurer Katze	eurem Haus
accusative	euren Freund	eure Katze	euer Haus

	plural
nominative	eure Freunde, Katzen, Häuser
dative	euren Freunden, Katzen, Häusern
accusative	eure Freunde, Katzen, Häuser

C. Kleider und Farben. *(Clothing and colors.)* Expand the following statements with a second sentence telling what color each item of clothing is that the following people are wearing. Use a possessive adjective in each sentence you write.

Beispiel Alex trägt ein Hemd. (rot)
➤ Sein Hemd ist rot.

Kleider (Clothes)

der Anzug *suit* (pl. die Anzüge)

die Bluse *blouse* (pl. die Blusen)

der Gürtel *belt* (pl. die Gürtel)

der Handschuh *glove*
(pl. die Handschuhe)

das Hemd *shirt* (pl. die Hemden)

die Hose *pair of pants*
(pl. die Hosen)

die Jacke *jacket* (pl. die Jacken)

die Jeans (plural) *jeans*

das Kleid *dress* (pl. die Kleider)

die Krawatte *necktie*
(pl. die Krawatten)

der Mantel *coat* (pl. die Mäntel)

der Pulli *sweater* (pl. die Pullis)

der Rock *skirt* (pl. die Röcke)

der Schuh *shoe* (pl. die Schuhe)

die Shorts (plural) *shorts*

die Socke *sock* (pl. die Socken)

der Stiefel *boot* (pl. die Stiefel)

der Strumpf *stocking*
(pl. die Strümpfe)

das T-shirt *T-shirt*
(pl. die T-Shirts)

der Turnschuh *sneaker*
(pl. die Turnschuhe)

Farben (Colors)

die Farbe *color* (pl. **die Farben**)	**grün** *green*
beige *beige*	**hell** *light*
blau *blue*	**hellblau** *light blue*
braun *brown*	**orange** *orange*
bunt *colorful*	**rosa** *pink*
dunkel *dark*	**rot** *red*
dunkelblau *dark blue*	**schwarz** *black*
gelb *yellow*	**weiß** *white*
grau *gray*	

1. Hildegard trägt einen Rock. (dunkelgrün)

   _____

2. Peter trägt Jeans. (blau)

   _____

3. Der Lehrer trägt eine Krawatte. (bunt)

   _____

4. Petra trägt Stiefel. (braun)

   _____

5. Franz und Felix tragen Turnschuhe. (weiß)

   _____

6. Du trägst eine Bluse. (gelb)

   _____

7. Wir tragen Shorts. (beige)

   _____

8. Ich trage eine Jacke. (grau)

   _____

D. Unsre Kleider. Create conversations about the colors of the clothing these friends are wearing.

Beispiel ich / Socken / dunkelblau / du / hellblau
> ➤ Meine Socken sind dunkelblau. Welche Farbe haben deine Socken?
> Meine Socken sind hellblau.

1. Dieter / Schuhe / schwarz / du / braun

_____

_____

_____

2. ich / Gürtel / weiß / du / beige

_____

_____

_____

3. wir / Kleid / grün / Sie / rot

_____

_____

_____

4. ich / Turnschuhe / schwarz / deine Freunde / weiß

_____

_____

_____

E. Gute Freunde. These friends lend each other the clothing they need. Say so using **leihen,** the correct dative pronoun, and the correct form of the possessive adjective.

Beispiel Paul hat keinen Gürtel. (Peter)
> ➤ Peter leiht ihm seinen Gürtel.

1. Wir haben keine Jeans. (Sabine und Sara)

_____

2. Ich habe keinen Anzug. (Lothar)

_____

3. Du hast keine Strümpfe. (Mutter)

_____

4. Herr Richter, Sie haben keine Krawatte. (ich)

_____

5. Ihr habt keine Stiefel. (wir)

_____

6. Andreas hat keine Handschuhe. (du)

_____

7. Ich habe keinen Pulli. (Birgit)

_____

F. Kleiderpflege. *(Caring for your clothing.)* Tell how the following people are taking care of their clothing (or not!). Use the appropriate possessive adjective in each sentence.

Beispiel   Christa / bügeln / Rock
       ➤ Christa bügelt ihren Rock.

Kleiderpflege	
bügeln *to iron*	**verlieren** *to lose*
kürzen *to shorten*	**waschen** (a > ä) *to wash*
nähen *to sew*	**zerreißen** *to tear*
putzen *to shine (shoes)*	

1. Vater / putzen / Schuhe

_____

2. ich / waschen / Hemd

_____

3. das Kind / zerreißen / Mantel

_____

➤➤➤➤➤

4. ihr / kürzen / Hosen

_____

5. Erika und Kirstin / waschen / Strümpfe

_____

6. meine Mutter / nähen / Bluse

_____

7. du / bügeln / Anzug

_____

8. wir / putzen / Stiefel

_____

III. Accusative Form of Pronouns

■ Study the accusative forms of the personal pronouns. Pay special attention to the difference between the dative and the accusative.

nominative	dative	accusative
ich	mir	mich
du	dir	dich
er	ihm	ihn
sie	ihr	sie
es	ihm	es
wir	uns	uns
ihr	euch	euch
sie	ihnen	sie
Sie	Ihnen	Sie

1. Remember that singular nouns in the accusative referring to things are replaced by **ihn, sie, es** according to their grammatical gender.

Bügelst du deinen Anzug.   _Are you ironing your suit?_
Ja, ich bügele ihn.   _Yes, I'm ironing it._

Wäschst du deine Bluse?   _Are you washing your blouse?_
Ja, ich wasche sie.   _Yes, I'm washing it._

Nähst du dein Hemd?   _Are you sewing your shirt?_
Ja, ich nähe es.   _Yes, I'm sewing it._

2. When there is a dative (indirect object) and an accusative noun (direct object) in a sentence, the dative precedes the accusative.

Wir schenken unsrem Lehrer das Buch.   _We're giving our teacher the book._

3. However, when a sentence has a dative and an accusative pronoun, the accusative precedes the dative.

Wir schenken es ihm. *We're giving it to him.*

4. When one object is a pronoun and the other a noun, the pronoun comes first, whether it's dative or accusative.

Wir schenken ihm das Buch. *We're giving him the book.*

Wir schenken es unsrem Lehrer. *We're giving it to our teacher.*

G. Nein, das nicht. Tell what these people are not doing with their clothing by answering the following questions in the negative, replacing the direct object noun with the appropriate object pronoun.

Beispiel Kauft Johann dieses Hemd?
➤ Nein, er kauft es nicht.

1. Putzt Karl seine Schuhe?

_____

2. Bügelst du dein Kleid?

_____

3. Tragen die Kinder ihre Turnschuhe?

_____

4. Wäschst du deinen Pulli?

_____

5. Verliert ihr eure Handschuhe oft?

_____

6. Brauchst du deinen Gürtel?

_____

7. Sucht Manfred seine Krawatte?

_____

8. Holst du deine Jacke?

_____

H. Wir helfen. Tell how we are going to help these people get what they want or need. Use the adjective and verb in parentheses and the appropriate accusative pronoun.

Beispiel Der Architekt braucht ein Büro. (gut / zeigen)
➤ Dieses Büro ist gut. Wir zeigen es dem Architekt.

1. Die Kinder brauchen Turnschuhe. (preiswert / kaufen)

     _____

2. Unser Onkel liest gern eine Zeitschrift. (interessant / schicken)

     _____

3. Die Nachbarn brauchen einen Taschenrechner. (nicht kaputt / leihen)

     _____

4. Die Studentin sucht einen Roman. (schön / empfehlen)

     _____

5. Unsre Mutter braucht eine Zeitung. (neu / bringen)

     _____

6. Unser Freund hat keine Krawatte. (bunt / schenken)

     _____

7. Den Nachbarn gefällt unser Auto. (alt / verkaufen)

     _____

8. Unser Sohn braucht einen Block. (groß / geben)

     _____

IV. Genitive (Possessive Ending in -s)

■ Possession can be shown in German by adding an **-s** (without an apostrophe) to a name:

Jürgens Stereoanlage	*Jürgen's stereo system*
Meikes Tonbandgerät	*Meike's tape recorder*

In many other cases, **von** + dative is used in everyday speech:

der Kassettenrekorder von meinem Bruder	*my brother's cassette recorder*
der Computer von meiner Mutter	*my mother's computer*

I. **Was hältst du davon?** *(What do you think of it?)* Tell what you think of the items mentioned using the words in parentheses, the verb **sein,** and the appropriate possessive construction.

Beispiel Jürgen hat eine Stereoanlage. (wunderbar)
    ➤ Jürgens Stereoanlage ist wunderbar.

Elektronische Geräte (Electronic equipment)

der CD-Spieler *CD player* (pl. **die CD-Spieler**)

das Fax *fax* (pl. **die Faxe**)

der Fernseher *TV set* (pl. **die Fernseher**)

der Fotoapparat *camera* (pl. **die Fotoapparate**)

der Fotokopierer *photocopier* (pl. **die Fotokopierer**)

das Radio *radio* (pl. **die Radios**)

die Satellitenschüssel *satellite dish* (pl. **die Satellitenschüsseln**)

die Stereoanlage *stereo system* (pl. **die Stereoanlagen**)

das Tonbandgerät *tape recorder* (pl. **die Tonbandgeräte**)

die Videokamera *video camera* (pl. **die Videokameras**)

der Videorekorder *VCR* (pl. **die Videorekorder**)

---

1. Katrin hat eine Videokamera. (zu teuer)

   _____

2. Die Nachbarn haben einen Videorekorder. (toll)

   _____

3. Josef hat einen Fernseher. (kaputt)

   _____

4. Die Lehrerin hat einen CD-Spieler. (preiswert)

   _____

5. Simone hat einen Fotoapparat. (nicht gut)

   _____

6. Mein Onkel hat eine Stereoanlage. (toll)

   _____

7. Das Büro hat einen Fotokopierer. (alt)

_____

8. Reinhard hat Tonbandgeräte. (kaputt)

_____

9. Meine Großeltern haben ein Radio. (sehr alt)

_____

10. Die Schule hat eine Satellitenschüssel. (prima)

_____

Fernsehen (Television)

- Television is assuming an ever more important role in German life as the medium expands with the growth of cable and satellite channels. Germans are currently receiving about 25 channels if they have cable or a satellite dish. The increasing number of channels means greater competition for the government-funded stations, which have been the backbone of the German television system. There are two national networks, ARD and ZDF, as well as state or regional channels, called third channels. There are also numerous private networks with very specific and excellent programming devoted to areas such as education, sports, health, and cultural events. All owners of TV sets and radios must pay a yearly user's fee to the government.
- German television programming includes some American TV shows and films. Some are dubbed into German; others are presented in English with German subtitles. Still others are broadcast in two-channel sound for people with stereo TV sets. These viewers can switch back and forth between the two languages. German cable offers CNN, NBC Super Channel, and the European edition of MTV.

J. **Und du?** Answer the following questions in complete sentences.

1. Was trägst du heute? Welche Farben haben deine Kleider?

   _____

2. Wo kaufst du deine Kleider?

   _____

3. Was für Geräte hast du in deinem Zimmer? Wie sind sie? Alt? Neu? Kaputt?

   _____

4. Hast du Kabelfernsehen oder eine Satellitenschüssel?

   _____

5. Was für Geräte gibt es in eurer Schule?

   _____

K. **Aufsatz.** Write an eight-sentence dialogue between two students at the beginning of the school year. To get to know each other better, they discuss their tastes in clothes, mentioning the articles of clothing and colors they like. They also talk about electronic equipment they like to use in their spare time. You can refer to the extra vocabulary in Exercises C and I.

Adjectives after *der* and *dieser*; Adjectives after *ein* and the Possessive Adjectives

I. Adjectives after *der* and *dieser*

■ In German, when an adjective follows a form of **sein,** it has no ending.

Das Buch ist interessant.	*The book is interesting.*
Diese Kleider sind neu.	*These clothes are new.*

When an adjective comes before a noun, it has endings to agree with the gender, number, and case of the noun. After a definite article or a form of **dieser,** the adjective has the ending **-en** in all forms except the nominative singular of all genders and the feminine and neuter accusative, where the adjective ends in **-e.**

	masculine	feminine
nominative	der/dieser gute Mann	die/diese gute Frau
dative	dem/diesem guten Mann	der/dieser guten Frau
accusative	den/diesen guten Mann	die/diese gute Frau

	neuter
nominative	das/dieses gute Kind
dative	dem/diesem guten Kind
accusative	das/dieses gute Kind

In the plural, all forms of the adjective end in **-en:**

nominative	die/diese guten Männer, Frauen, Kinder
dative	den/diesen guten Männern, Frauen, Kindern
accusative	die/diese guten Männer, Frauen, Kinder

■ Another word that functions like the definite article or **dieser** is the interrogative **welcher** (*which*). Adjectives following **welcher** have the same endings as when they follow the definite article.

In welchem neuen Gebäude arbeitet sie?	*In which new building does she work?*

■ Note the following changes in the stem of certain adjectives:

Adjectives ending in **-el** and adjectives with a base such as **-auer** and **-euer** drop the **e** before an ending:

in einer dunklen Straße

ein teures Kleid

die saure Milch

A. Ja, diese. Answer each of the following questions in the affirmative, adding the adjective in parentheses in its proper form.

Beispiel Liest du diese Zeitschrift? (interessant)
> ➤ Ja, ich lese diese interessante Zeitschrift.

1. Trägst du dieses Hemd? (weiß)

   _____

2. Kaufst du ein in diesem Laden? (modern)

   _____

3. Arbeiten sie in diesem Zimmer? (dunkel)

   _____

4. Spricht dieser Lehrer Deutsch? (klug)

   _____

5. Öffnest du diese Fenster? (groß)

   _____

6. Gefällt dir diese Wohnung? (schön)

   _____

7. Besuchen wir diesen Betrieb? (riesig)

   _____

8. Hilft die Lehrerin diesem Studenten? (fleißig)

   _____

B. Leute. *(People.)* Fill in the missing forms of the definite article and the adjectives in parentheses to produce descriptions of the people.

> ## Leute (People)
>
> | | |
> |---|---|
> | **ärgerlich** *annoying* | **hübsch** *pretty* |
> | **arm** *poor* | **jung** *young* |
> | **begabt** *talented* | **kräftig** *strong* |
> | **berühmt** *famous* | **reich** *rich* |
> | **dumm** *stupid* | **schwach** *weak* |
> | **geschickt, fähig** *capable, skillful* | |

1. Unser Nachbar ist Schriftsteller.

    a. (begabt)   _____ Schriftsteller schreibt
        Romane und Gedichte.

    b. (berühmt)   Wir sprechen oft mit _____
        Schriftsteller.

    c. (interessant) Wir sehen _____ Schriftsteller
        jeden Tag.

2. Bergmanns haben kein Geld.

    a. (arm)   Wir helfen _____ Familie.

    b. (klug)   Wir schenken _____ Kindern
        Bücher.

    c. (traurig)   _____ Vater braucht Arbeit.

3. Die Lehrerin hat viele Studenten.

    a. (fleißig)   Sie hat _____ Studenten gern.

    b. (begabt)   Sie hilft _____ Studenten.

    c. (faul)   _____ Studenten gefallen ihr nicht.

4. Monika Fiedler ist Geschäftsfrau.

    a. (reich)   _____ Geschäftsfrau hat ein Büro
        in diesem Gebäude.

    b. (jung)   Wir sprechen oft mit _____
        Geschäftsfrau.

    c. (fähig)   Alle Leute grüßen _____
        Geschäftsfrau.

C. Stadtbummel. What are these tourists visiting in Düsseldorf? Complete the following sentences with the appropriate form of the definite article and adjective to find out.

1. (modern)   Die Touristen besuchen _____ Stadtmitte.

2. (schön)   Ich suche _____ Kaufhäuser.

3. (groß)   Markus liest in _____ Bibliothek.

4. (ruhig)   Du besuchst _____ Park.

5. (neu)   Die Kinder schwimmen in _____ Schwimmbad.

6. (berühmt)   _____ Kunstmuseum gefällt uns gut.

7. (alt)   Wir haben _____ Brücken gern.

8. (riesig)   Wir finden _____ Dom sehr interessant.

Die Künste in Deutschland (The arts in Germany)

- **Literature**
  Germany has produced some internationally celebrated writers in the 20th century, among them the novelists Thomas Mann, who won the Nobel Prize for literature in 1929, and Heinrich Böll, who won it in 1972. Günter Grass, also a novelist, is the most recent German recipient of the Nobel Prize for literature, which he was awarded in 1999.

- **Museums**
  Germany houses some of the greatest art treasures in the world. Important works by famous German artists such as Holbein the Younger and the Older and Dürer, as well as other universally acclaimed artists, can be seen in small towns, castles, churches, and cathedrals, as well as in major cities. Among the most famous museums are the **Pergamon Museum** in Berlin, the **Gemäldegalerie** in Dresden, the **Wallraf-Richartz Museum/Ludwig Museum** in Cologne, and the **Alte Pinakothek** and **Neue Pinakothek** in Munich. Munich is also the home of perhaps the most visited museum in Germany and one of the most famous science and technology museums in the world: the **Deutsches Museum.**

- **Music**
  Many of the world's most famous composers were born in Germany: Beethoven, Brahms, Bach, Handel, Mendelssohn, Schumann, Wagner, Richard Strauss, Telemann, and Hindemith.

D. Unzufrieden im Restaurant. Use **dieser** + adjective to express this customer's complaints about the food.

Beispiel kalt / Suppe / essen
➤ Diese kalte Suppe esse ich nicht.

Wie ist das Essen?

bitter *bitter*	**sauer** *sour*
frisch *fresh*	**scharf** *spicy*
heiß *hot*	**schlecht** *bad*
kalt *cold*	**süß** *sweet*
kühl *cool*	**trocken** *dry*
lecker *tasty, delicious*	**warm** *warm*
salzig *salty*	

---

1. alt / Rindfleisch / essen

   _____

2. kalt / Kaffee / trinken

   _____

3. sauer / Orangensaft / trinken

   _____

4. bitter / Gemüse / essen

   _____

5. trocken / Fisch / essen

   _____

6. alt / Brot / essen

   _____

7. schlecht / Tee / trinken

   _____

8. salzig / Käse / essen

   _____

E. Studenten vom Ausland. *(Foreign students.)* Note that the names of languages that you learned are also adjectives of nationality: **eine deutsche Stadt** (*a German city*). Tell what the nationality of each of these foreign students is by the language he or she speaks. Adjectives of nationality are not capitalized in German.

Beispiel Studentin / Deutsch
  ➤ Diese deutsche Studentin spricht Deutsch.

1. Student / Chinesisch

_____

2. Studentin / Englisch

_____

3. Student / Französisch

_____

4. Studentin / Italienisch

_____

5. Student / Japanisch

_____

6. Studentin / Russisch

_____

7. Student / Spanisch

_____

F. Ja, das tun wir. *(Yes, we'll do that.)* Answer the following questions with a noun or pronoun in the dative case. Use the definite article and the adjective given in the question.

Beispiel Der Lehrer ist streng. Gehorcht ihr ihm?
  ➤ Ja, dem strengen Lehrer gehorchen wir.

1. Der Polizist ist nett. Folgt ihr ihm?

_____

2. Der Student ist arm. Helft ihr ihm?

_____

➤➤➤➤➤

3. Die Frau ist alt. Schreibt ihr ihr?

_____

4. Der Junge ist klug. Gratuliert ihr ihm zum Geburtstag?

_____

5. Der Architekt ist geschickt. Antwortet ihr ihm?

_____

6. Die Kinder sind traurig. Lest ihr ihnen eine Geschichte vor?

_____

II. Adjectives after *ein* and the Possessive Adjectives

- Adjectives that follow the indefinite article or a possessive adjective have the same endings as adjectives after the definite article and **dieser** except for three cases. Contrast these forms:

	masculine singular, nominative	neuter singular, nominative and accusative
after **der**	der/dieser schöne Garten	das/dieses schöne Haus
after **ein**	ein/mein schöner Garten	ein/mein schönes Haus

Here is a summary of the forms of the adjective after **ein** and the possessive adjectives:

	singular		
	masculine	**feminine**	**neuter**
nominative	ein guter Mann	eine gute Frau	ein gutes Kind
dative	einem guten Mann	einer guten Frau	einem guten Kind
accusative	einen guten Mann	eine gute Frau	ein gutes Kind

	plural
nominative	meine schönen Gärten, Blumen, Kleider
dative	meinen schönen Gärten, Blumen, Kleidern
accusative	meine schönen Gärten, Blumen, Kleider

G. Was trägt man heute? Tell what the following people are wearing to school today. Use the appropriate possessive adjective and the correct form of the adjective in parentheses.

Beispiel   Jutta / Rock / (grün)
➤ Jutta trägt ihren grünen Rock.

Wie sind die Kleider? (How are the clothes?)

fesch *stylish, smart*	**modisch** *fashionable*
lang *long*	**schick** *smart-looking*

---

1. Gregor / Turnschuhe / (neu)

   _____

2. Gabi und Trudi / Röcke / (lang)

   _____

3. der Lehrer / Krawatte / (modisch)

   _____

4. ich / Hemd / (schick)

   _____

5. du / T-Shirt / (fesch)

   _____

6. Susi / Mantel / (hellblau)

   _____

7. ihr / Schuhe / (braun)

   _____

8. wir / Jacken / (schön)

   _____

H. Schulbesuch. *(A visit to the school.)* You're taking a new student around the school. Point things out to him or her by completing the following sentences with the indefinite article and the adjective and noun given.

Beispiel   Die Lehrer haben hier _____.
(klein / Lehrerzimmer)

➤ Die Lehrer haben hier ein kleines Lehrerzimmer.

Wir beschreiben die Schule

bequem *comfortable*   **still** *still, quiet*

laut *loud*   **toll** *great, terrific, awesome*

ruhig *quiet, peaceful*   **unbequem** *uncomfortable*

sauber *clean*

---

1. Hier gibt es _____.
   (groß / Sekretariat)

2. Die Schule hat _____.
   (sauber / Mensa)

3. Da links gibt es _____.
   (modern / Turnhalle)

4. Aber wir haben _____.
   (alt / Schwimmbad)

5. Wir lernen in _____.
   (bequem / Hörsaal)

6. Wir hören Tonbänder in _____.
   (toll / Sprachlabor)

7. Die Schule hat hier _____.
   (ruhig / Bibliothek)

8. Dort drüben gibt es _____.
   (riesig / Fußballstadion)

I. Ja, das ist er. Answer each of the following questions using the indefinite article and the adjective in the question. Remember to change the form of the adjective when you place it before the noun.

Beispiel   Ist dieser Lehrer streng?
➤ Ja, er ist ein strenger Lehrer.

der **Film** *film, movie* (pl. **die Filme**)

der **Kerl** *fellow* (pl. **die Kerle** or **die Kerls**)

das **Lied** *song* (pl. **die Lieder**)

der **Sänger** *male singer* (pl. **die Sänger**)

die **Sängerin** *female singer* (pl. **die Sängerinnen**)

beliebt *popular*	**naß** *wet*
billig *cheap*	**streng** *strict*
blöd *dumb, stupid*	**teuer** *expensive*
köstlich *delicious*	**wichtig** *important*
lustig *funny*	

1. Ist dieser Artikel wichtig?

   _____

2. Ist dieses Lied beliebt?

   _____

3. Ist dieses Tonbandgerät billig?

   _____

4. Ist dieser Kerl blöd?

   _____

5. Ist dieser Käse köstlich?

   _____

6. Ist dieser Film lustig?

   _____

7. Ist diese Sängerin begabt?

   _____

8. Ist diese Stereoanlage teuer?

   _____

J. Leider haben wir das nicht. These students aren't having too much luck shopping today. Write sentences, using the correct forms of the adjective and noun given.

Beispiel schwarz / Schultasche
➤ Ich brauche eine schwarze Schultasche.
   Leider haben wir keine schwarzen Schultaschen.

1. groß / Block

_____

_____

2. preiswert / Taschenrechner

_____

_____

3. billig / Heft

_____

_____

4. grün / Rock

_____

_____

5. braun / Anzug

_____

_____

6. kurz / Jacke

_____

_____

7. scharf / Wurst

_____

_____

8. deutsch / Zeitung

_____

_____

K. Das Haus. Show someone around your house. Describe each room by completing the sentences with the adjectives and nouns given.

Das Haus

Note: nouns ending in **-zimmer** do not change in the plural.

das Arbeitszimmer *study*

das Badezimmer *bathroom*

der Dachboden *attic* (pl. **die Dachböden**)

das Eßzimmer *dining room*

der Keller *cellar, basement* (pl. **die Keller**)

die Küche *kitchen* (pl. **die Küchen**)

das Schlafzimmer *bedroom*

das Wohnzimmer *living room*

---

1. Wir essen in _____.
   (unsre / groß / Küche)

2. Oben haben wir _____.
   (ein / klein / Dachboden)

3. _____ ist für die Kinder ein
   Spielzimmer. (unser / groß / Keller)

4. Wir sitzen oft in _____.
   (das / bequem / Wohnzimmer)

5. Unser Haus hat _____.
   (ein / modern / Badezimmer)

6. Wir schlafen gut in _____.
   (das / ruhig / Schlafzimmer)

7. Vater hat ein Telefon in _____.
   (sein / toll / Arbeitszimmer)

8. Wir haben einen großen Tisch in _____.
   (unser / schön / Eßzimmer)

L. Und du? Answer the following questions in complete sentences. Try to use at least one adjective in each answer.

1. Was für eine Schultasche hast du?

   _____

2. Wie ist dein(e) Deutschlehrer(in)?

   _____

3. Mit wem ißt du in der Mensa?

   _____

4. Wem hilfst du gern?

   _____

5. Was für ein T-Shirt trägst du gern?

   _____

M. Aufsatz. Describe your house or apartment. Use adjectives in each sentence to describe the rooms and features.

Modals: mögen, müssen, wollen, dürfen, können, sollen

I. Modals: *mögen, müssen, wollen*

■ Modal verbs usually occur with an infinitive and indicate the attitude of the subject toward the action of the infinitive: desire, obligation, ability, etc. The modal auxiliary verbs are **mögen, müssen, wollen, dürfen, können,** and **sollen.** All modals except **sollen** have a different vowel in the singular from the vowel of the infinitive. Study the conjugation of **mögen, müssen,** and **wollen.**

MÖGEN *TO LIKE*	**MÜSSEN** *MUST, HAVE TO*	**WOLLEN** *TO WANT*
ich **mag**	ich **muß**	ich **will**
du **magst**	du **mußt**	du **willst**
er/sie/es **mag**	er/sie/es **muß**	er/sie/es **will**
wir **mögen**	wir **müssen**	wir **wollen**
ihr **mögt**	ihr **müßt**	ihr **wollt**
sie **mögen**	sie **müssen**	sie **wollen**
Sie **mögen**	Sie **müssen**	Sie **wollen**

1. Note the difference in form between **du mußt** and **ihr müßt.**

2. Modal verbs do not add **-t** in the third-person singular (**er/sie/es**) form, nor do they have **-e** in the **ich** form.

3. Modals are commonly used with an infinitive.

Wir müssen arbeiten.	*We have to work.*
Ich will bummeln.	*I want to walk around.*

4. If other elements are present, they go between the modal and the infinitive.

Wir müssen heute arbeiten.	*We have to work today.*
Ich will mit dir jetzt bummeln.	*I want to walk around with you now.*

5. **Mögen** often has nouns as direct objects, especially nouns referring to foods, places, and people.

Magst du Tee? Nein, ich mag Kaffee.	*Do you like tea? No, I like coffee.*
Sie mag die Stadt nicht.	*She doesn't like the city.*
Sie mögen ihren Lehrer.	*They like their teacher.*

6. A subjunctive conjugation of **mögen** is more common than the simple present. Here are the forms.

ich **möchte**	wir **möchten**
du **möchtest**	ihr **möchtet**
er/sie/es **möchte**	sie **möchten**

Ich möchte ein Glas Limonade. *I'd like a glass of soda.*

Wir möchten dieses Jahr nach Deutschland fahren. *We'd like to go to Germany this year.*

A. Welches Subjekt? Check all of the possible subjects with which the verb forms can be used.

1. mußt

   ich ___ du ___ er ___ wir ___ ihr ___ die Studenten ___ Sie ___

2. will

   ich ___ du ___ er ___ wir ___ ihr ___ die Studenten ___ Sie ___

3. wollen

   ich ___ du ___ er ___ wir ___ ihr ___ die Studenten ___ Sie ___

4. mögen

   ich ___ du ___ er ___ wir ___ ihr ___ die Studenten ___ Sie ___

5. mögt

   ich ___ du ___ er ___ wir ___ ihr ___ die Studenten ___ Sie ___

6. müssen

   ich ___ du ___ er ___ wir ___ ihr ___ die Studenten ___ Sie ___

7. möchtest

   ich ___ du ___ er ___ wir ___ ihr ___ die Studenten ___ Sie ___

8. müßt

   ich ___ du ___ er ___ wir ___ ihr ___ die Studenten ___ Sie ___

9. mag

   ich ___ du ___ er ___ wir ___ ihr ___ die Studenten ___ Sie ___

10. muß

   ich ___ du ___ er ___ wir ___ ihr ___ die Studenten ___ Sie ___

B. Gute Ratschläge. *(Good advice.)* One friend tells another what he or she doesn't want to do. The other says that he or she must do it. Create their dialogues using **wollen** and **müssen.**

Beispiel (studieren)
> Ich will nicht studieren.
> Aber du mußt studieren.

1. arbeiten

_____

_____

2. antworten

_____

_____

3. fragen

_____

_____

4. schreiben

_____

_____

5. bleiben

_____

_____

6. essen

_____

_____

7. gehen

_____

_____

➤➤➤➤➤

8. spielen

_____

_____

C. Bei Tisch. *(At the table.)* Create conversations in which one person offers food or drink with **möchte** and the other declines with **Ich will kein +** **essen** or **trinken.**

Beispiel Brot
   ➤ Möchten Sie Brot?
     Nein, danke. Ich will kein Brot essen.

1. Milch

_____

_____

2. Apfelmuß

_____

_____

3. Bonbons

_____

_____

4. Orangensaft

_____

_____

5. Wurst

_____

_____

6. Tee

_____

_____

7. Suppe

_____

_____

8. Eis

_____

_____

D. Über Geschmack läßt sich nicht streiten. *(There's no accounting for taste.)* Tell your friend that the reason the following people are not eating these foods is that they don't like them.

Beispiel Warum ißt Johann den Käse nicht?
➢ Er mag keinen Käse.

1. Warum eßt ihr den Fisch nicht?

_____

2. Warum ißt du den Reis nicht?

_____

3. Warum ißt Ulrike das Kalbfleisch nicht?

_____

4. Warum essen die Kinder den Schinken nicht?

_____

5. Warum trinkt Moritz den Kaffee nicht?

_____

6. Warum ißt Birgit die Kartoffeln nicht?

_____

7. Warum trinkst du die Limonade nicht?

_____

8. Warum essen Sie die Pizza nicht?

_____

E. Gespräche. Complete these conversations. Two friends are talking. The first gives some information. Using the material in parentheses, the second friend tells the first one what he or she must do. The first friend replies that he or she does not want to do it.

Beispiel Dieser Roman ist langweilig. (du / diesen Roman lesen)
> ➤ Du mußt diesen Roman lesen.
> Ich will ihn nicht lesen.

Menschen und Aufgaben (People and assignments)

fehlen: in der Schule fehlen
to be absent from school

höflich *polite*

leicht *easy*

die Notizen *notes*

rufen *to call*

schwierig *difficult*

---

1. Meine Schwester ist müde. (du / das Haus putzen)

_____

_____

2. Hans ist faul. (er / dem Nachbarn helfen)

_____

_____

3. Die Übungen sind schwierig. (du / die Hausaufgaben machen)

_____

_____

4. Der Junge ist nicht höflich. (er / dem Touristen antworten)

_____

_____

5. Magda fehlt in der Schule. (du / ihr deine Notizen leihen)

_____

_____

6. Ich habe Bauchschmerzen. (du / den Arzt anrufen)

_____

_____

7. Unser Sohn hat unser altes Auto gern. (ihr / ihm das alte Auto geben)

_____

_____

F. Schlecht gelaunt. *(In a bad mood.)* Today nobody wants to do anything. Use **nicht wollen** to tell what these people don't want to do.

Beispiel Karl / arbeiten
➤ Karl will nicht arbeiten.

1. wir / im Restaurant essen

_____

2. ihr / diese Lieder hören

_____

3. die Studenten / in der Bibliothek lesen

_____

4. du / heute fahren

_____

5. unsre Freunde / den neuen Film sehen

_____

6. ich / meinen Anzug bügeln

_____

7. die Kinder / das Gemüse essen

_____

8. wir / den Hund füttern

_____

II. Modals: *dürfen, können, sollen*

DÜRFEN *MAY,* *TO BE ALLOWED TO*	KÖNNEN *CAN,* *TO BE ABLE TO*	SOLLEN *TO BE SUPPOSED TO*
ich **darf**	ich **kann**	ich **soll**
du **darfst**	du **kannst**	du **sollst**
er/sie/es **darf**	er/sie/es **kann**	er/sie/es **soll**
wir **dürfen**	wir **können**	wir **sollen**
ihr **dürft**	ihr **könnt**	ihr **sollt**
sie **dürfen**	sie **können**	sie **sollen**
Sie **dürfen**	Sie **können**	Sie **sollen**

1. **Dürfen** is the equivalent of English *may.*

   Darf ich das Fenster öffnen?   *May I open the window?*

2. In the negative, **dürfen** means *shouldn't, ought not, must not.*

   Ihr dürft eure Hefte nicht verlieren.   *You mustn't lose your notebooks.*

   Note that **muß nicht** means *doesn't have to.*

   Du mußt die Kleider nicht waschen.   *You don't have to wash the clothes.*

3. **Können** expresses *ability,* like English *can* or *be able.*

   Sie können das heute kaufen.   *You can buy that today.*

   Der Lehrer kann dir ein Buch empfehlen.   *The teacher can recommend a book to you.*

   Lothar kann seine Schultasche nicht finden.   *Lothar can't find his schoolbag.*

4. **Können** can express *possibility.*

   Das kann sein.   *That may be.*

   Die Prüfung kann schwierig sein.   *The text can be/may be hard.*

5. **Können** can mean *to know* or *to speak* with names of languages. The implication is to know through study.

   Hier können alle Deutsch.   *Everyone here knows how to speak German.*

6. **Sollen** means *to be supposed to.*

   Was soll ich tun?   *What am I supposed to do?*

   Mit wem soll ich gehen?   *With whom am I supposed to go?*

G. Welches Subjekt? Check all of the possible subjects with which the verb forms can be used.

1. sollt

   ich ___ du ___ er ___ wir ___ ihr ___ die Kinder ___ Sie ___

2. kannst

   ich ___ du ___ er ___ wir ___ ihr ___ die Kinder ___ Sie ___

3. könnt

   ich ___ du ___ er ___ wir ___ ihr ___ die Kinder ___ Sie ___

4. kann

   ich ___ du ___ er ___ wir ___ ihr ___ die Kinder ___ Sie ___

5. sollen

   ich ___ du ___ er ___ wir ___ ihr ___ die Kinder ___ Sie ___

6. darfst

   ich ___ du ___ er ___ wir ___ ihr ___ die Kinder ___ Sie ___

7. darf

   ich ___ du ___ er ___ wir ___ ihr ___ die Kinder ___ Sie ___

8. können

   ich ___ du ___ er ___ wir ___ ihr ___ die Kinder ___ Sie ___

9. dürft

   ich ___ du ___ er ___ wir ___ ihr ___ die Kinder ___ Sie ___

H. Was sollen sie tun? Ask what these people are supposed to do in each case.

Beispiel   Marie hat eine Prüfung. (was / lernen)
    ➤ Was soll sie lernen?

1. Günter ist heute krank. (wer / den Arzt anrufen)

   _____

2. Elfriede hat Hunger. (was / essen)

   _____

3. Meine Freunde wollen nach Berlin fahren. (wie / fahren)

   _____

➤➤➤➤➤

4. Morgen ißt du bei uns. (um wieviel Uhr / kommen)

_____

5. Heute gehen wir ins Kino. (welchen Film / sehen)

_____

6. Wir sollen um sechs Uhr essen. (wo / essen)

_____

7. Morgen haben wir eine Feier. (was / tragen)

_____

8. Du mußt etwas zu der Feier bringen. (was / kaufen)

_____

I. Nicht können. Tell what things the following people can't do.

Beispiel   Klaus / schwimmen
              ➢ Klaus kann nicht schwimmen.

Beschäftigungen (Activities)

kochen _to cook_

die Stadt besichtigen _to visit the city_

tanzen _to dance_

---

1. meine Schwester / kochen

_____

2. Robert / tanzen

_____

3. ich / die Katze füttern

_____

4. wir / ein Geschenk für unsre Mutter finden

_____

5. die Touristen / die Stadt besichtigen

_____

6. wir / diese Suppe essen

_____

7. du / nähen

_____

8. ihr / auf Deutsch schreiben

_____

Feste feiern (Celebrations)

- In Germany, the person who has the birthday is the one who treats his or her friends. The birthday celebrant is expected to invite his or her friends to a restaurant to celebrate the occasion. Guests are expected to bring a gift. Birthday presents are not given before the actual birthday for superstitious reasons.
- **Sylvester,** or New Year's Eve, is celebrated by going to a party or a restaurant. At midnight, fireworks are set off in the streets.
- **Rosenmontag** (Monday before Lent) is usually the day for the **Karneval** parades. Floats, costumed participants, and marching bands make their way through the streets. After the parade, people often go to **Karneval** parties. **Karneval** is celebrated mostly by Catholics in Germany, especially in the Rhineland and Bavaria. The largest celebrations are in Cologne, Munich, Düsseldorf, and Mainz.

J. Darf ich? Ask for permission for these people to do the following things.

Beispiel   Ihnen helfen / wir
     ➤ Dürfen wir Ihnen helfen?

1. hier spielen / die Kinder

_____

2. jetzt gehen / ich

_____

3. mit Ihnen reden / wir

_____

➤➤➤➤➤

4. dir diese Blumen schenken / ich

_____

5. dir diesen Brief zeigen / wir

_____

6. mit euch fahren / ich

_____

7. deine Notizen sehen / wir

_____

K. Und du? Answer the following questions in complete sentences.

1. Was möchtest du am Samstag tun? Und deine Freunde?

_____

2. Kannst du gut schwimmen? Tanzen?

_____

3. Um wieviel Uhr mußt du samstags nach Hause kommen? Und deine Freunde?

_____

4. Was sollst du heute tun? Was willst du tun?

_____

5. Brauchst du Kleider? Was willst du kaufen?

_____

L. Aufsatz. Write a paragraph of five or six sentences in which you tell about your plans for the weekend. Tell what you want to do, what you can or cannot do, and what you are supposed to do. Include the phrase **dieses Wochenende** (_this weekend_) in your first sentence.

Verbs with Separable Prefixes; Verbs with Inseparable Prefixes; Negative and Indefinite Words

I. Verbs with Separable Prefixes

■ Many German verbs consist of a prefix and the verb stem:

anfangen *to begin* (**an** + **fangen; er fängt an**)

anhaben *to wear, have on* (**an** + **haben**)

ankommen *to arrive* (**an** + **kommen**)

anprobieren *to try on (an article of clothing)* (**an** + **probieren**)

anrufen *to call (on the phone)* (**an** + **rufen**)

anziehen *to put on (an article of clothing)* (**an** + **ziehen**)

■ In the present tense, the prefix is separated from the verb and is placed after it at the end of the sentence.

Was ziehst du an?	*What are you putting on?*
Wann kommen sie an?	*When are they arriving?*
Wen rufst du an?	*Whom are you calling?*

■ All sentence elements stand between the verb and its prefix when the prefix is moved to the end of the sentence.

Ich komme an.	*I'm arriving.*
Ich komme morgen an.	*I'm arriving tomorrow.*
Ich komme morgen mit dem Zug an.	*I'm arriving tomorrow by train.*
Ich komme morgen um zwei Uhr mit dem Zug an.	*I'm arriving tomorrow at two by train.*

■ Some frequently used combinations of verbs and nouns function as if the noun were a separable prefix.

Auto fahren *to drive*

Rad fahren *to ride a bicycle, go bicycle riding*

Schlittschuh laufen *to ice skate*

Ski laufen *to ski*

„**Lauft ihr oft Ski?**"	*"Do you often go skiing?"*
„**Nein, aber wir laufen jeden Tag Schlittschuh.**"	*"No, but we go ice skating every day."*
„**Die Schule ist weit weg. Ich muß Rad fahren.**"	*"The school is far away. I have to go by bicycle."*
„**Wir können zusammen Rad fahren.**"	*"We can cycle together."*

- Here are some other verbs with separable prefixes. The prefixes are underlined.

<u>ab</u>holen *to get, pick up a person or a thing*

<u>ab</u>stellen *to turn off*

<u>an</u>halten *to stop*

<u>an</u>stellen *to turn on*

<u>auf</u>hören *to stop*

<u>auf</u>machen *to open*

<u>auf</u>nehmen *to record*

<u>auf</u>räumen *to clean up, straighten up*

<u>auf</u>stehen *to get up*

<u>aus</u>geben *to spend (money)*

<u>aus</u>packen *to unpack*

<u>aus</u>sehen *to look like*

<u>aus</u>steigen *to get off*

<u>aus</u>ziehen *to take off an article of clothing*

<u>ein</u>kaufen *to shop, to shop for*

<u>ein</u>laden *to invite*

<u>ein</u>packen *to pack*

<u>ein</u>steigen *to get in, get on (a vehicle)*

<u>fern</u>sehen *to watch television*

<u>mit</u>bringen *to bring along*

<u>mit</u>kommen *to come along*

<u>mit</u>nehmen *to take along*

<u>vor</u>haben *to plan, intend to*

<u>vor</u>schlagen *to suggest* (er schlägt vor)

<u>zu</u>machen *to close*

<u>zurück</u>bringen *to bring back*

<u>zurück</u>fahren *to drive back*

<u>zurück</u>geben *to give back*

<u>zurück</u>gehen *to go back*

<u>zurück</u>kommen *to come back*

<u>zusammen</u>kommen *to get together*

A. Ein Flug. *(A flight.)* Write sentences from the elements given to tell what the passengers on this flight do when they get to the airport.

Beispiel Flugzeug / ankommen
➤ Das Flugzeug kommt an.

Ein Flug

das elektrische Gerät *electrical appliance* (pl. **die elektrische Geräte**)

der Flug *flight* (pl. **die Flüge**)

das Gepäck *baggage*

heute in einer Woche *a week from today*

der Koffer *suitcase* (pl. **die Koffer**)

der Passagier *passenger* (pl. **die Passagiere**)

der/die Verwandte *relative* (pl. **die Verwandten**)

---

1. Die Passagiere / alle elektrischen Geräte / abstellen

   _____

2. Die Passagiere / aufstehen

   _____

3. sie / aussteigen

   _____

4. Die Passagiere / das Gepäck / abholen

   _____

5. sie / ihre Koffer / mitnehmen

   _____

6. sie / die Mäntel / anziehen

   _____

7. sie / ihre Verwandten und Freunden / anrufen

   _____

8. Die Passagiere / heute in einer Woche / zurückfahren

   _____

B. Winterurlaub. What are these young people doing on their winter vacation? Create sentences from the elements given to find out.

Beispiel   Die jungen Leute / in dem Hotel / ankommen
          ➤ Die jungen Leute kommen in dem Hotel an.

1. alle Menschen / die Koffer / auspacken

   _____

2. Joachim und Rudi / den ganzen Tag / Ski laufen

   _____

3. Ute und Gottfried / stundenlang zusammen / Schlittschuh laufen

   _____

➤➤➤➤➤

4. die kleinen Kinder / ihre Mäntel / anziehen

_____

5. der faule Wilhelm / den Fernseher / anstellen

_____

6. er / den ganzen Tag / fernsehen

_____

7. die arme Hilde / ihren Koffer / einpacken

_____

8. sie / morgen um zwölf Uhr / zurückfahren

_____

C. Ein Tagesausflug. *(A day trip.)* A group of friends is making plans for a day trip. Write the questions they ask each other.

Beispiel mitkommen / wer / wollen
➤ Wer will mitkommen?

1. einladen / sollen / wir / wen

_____

2. anrufen / können / wer / alle unsre Freunde

_____

3. ausgeben / dürfen / wir / wieviel Geld

_____

4. mitbringen / müssen / wir / was

_____

5. anhaben / sollen / wir / was

_____

6. Rad fahren / können / wir / wann

_____

7. vorschlagen / können / du / was

_____

8. zurückkommen / sollen / wir / wann

_____

D. Axel muß fleißig sein. *(Axel has to work hard.)* What does Axel's mother tell him to do in order to be sure he gets his homework done? Use **du** + the correct form of the modal given to write what she tells him.

Beispiel müssen / sofort nach der Schule / zurückkommen
    ➤ Du mußt sofort nach der Schule zurückkommen.

1. dürfen / deine Freunde / nicht / anrufen

_____

2. müssen / mit dem Plaudern / aufhören

_____

3. sollen / deine Turnschuhe / ausziehen

_____

4. sollen / deine Schultasche / auspacken

_____

5. sollen / deine Bücher / aufmachen

_____

6. sollen / deine Hausaufgaben / anfangen

_____

7. dürfen / den Fernseher / nicht / anstellen

_____

8. können / nicht / fernsehen

_____

E. Gespräche. *(Conversations.)* Create dialogues in which two friends are planning a get-together. Use the infinitive of the verb and the modal in the question, but drop the modal and use only the conjugated verb in the response. Some dialogues will have information questions, others yes/no questions.

Beispiel du / wollen / mitkommen
> ➤ Willst du mitkommen?
>   Ja, ich komme mit.

Wir kommen zusammen

anders *else*

das Essen *food*

etwas *something;* **etwas anderes** *something else*

das Fußballspiel *soccer game* (pl. **die Fußballspiele**)

das Geld *money*

die Mark *mark* (unit of currency in Germany)

das Spiel *game* (pl. **die Spiele**)

---

1. wo / wir / sollen / einkaufen / das Essen // im Supermarkt

   _____

   _____

2. wieviel Geld / wir / können / ausgeben // dreißig Mark

   _____

   _____

3. du / können / mitbringen / deine Tonbänder

   _____

   Ja, _____

4. wir / sollen / einladen / Konrad

   _____

   Ja, _____

5. du / können / anrufen / ihn

_____

Ja, _____

6. du / können / vorschlagen / etwas anderes

_____

Ja, _____

7. wir / sollen / aufnehmen / das Fußballspiel

_____

Ja, _____

Deutsches Geld

Germany is a member of the European Union, which has officially endorsed the euro as the currency of its member nations. Euro bills and coins will replace the Deutschmark and other European currencies by the year 2002.

II. Verbs with Inseparable Prefixes

■ Many verbal prefixes in German are inseparable. These are unstressed in the infinitive form. Often the meaning of a verb with an inseparable prefix cannot be predicted from the root verb. The most common inseparable prefixes are: **be-, emp-, ent-, er-, ge-, ver-,** and **zer-.** Compare the following pairs of verbs:

fallen, gefallen _to fall, to like_

fehlen, empfehlen _to be missing, to recommend_

lassen, verlassen _to allow, to leave_

schreiben, beschreiben _to write, to describe_

stehen, verstehen _to stand, to understand_

suchen, besuchen _to look for, to visit_

zählen, erzählen _to count, to tell (a story)_

■ Some common verbs with inseparable prefixes:

bedeuten *to mean, signify*

begleiten *to accompany*

begrüßen *to greet*

bekommen *to get, receive*

besprechen *to discuss*

bestellen *to order*

bezahlen *to pay*

erledigen *to take care of (chores, errands)*

erklären *to explain*

verbessern *to improve*

verbringen *to spend (time)*

vergessen *to forget* (**er vergißt**)

verpassen *to miss (an event, a train)*

verschwenden *to waste*

versuchen *to try, attempt*

zerschneiden *to cut up (into pieces)*

zerstören *to destroy*

F. Junge Leute helfen. *(Young people help out.)* A group of friends has decided to fix up an old, neglected neighborhood park. Construct sentences out of the elements given to find out exactly what they're doing.

Beispiel   heute / die Freunde / etwas Besonderes / versuchen
➤ Heute versuchen die Freunde etwas Besonderes.

Man arbeitet im Park

alle *all, everyone* (takes plural verb)

besonder *special*

das Ereignis *event* (pl. **die Ereignisse**)

die Harke *rake* (pl. **die Harken**)

niemand *nobody*

der Plan *plan* (pl. **die Pläne**)

die Schaufel *shovel* (pl. **die Schaufeln**)

wunderbar *wonderful*

---

1. sie / vorhaben / etwas Wunderbares

_____

2. sie / wollen / den alten Park / aufräumen

_____

3. sie / ihre Pläne / erklären

_____

4. alle / ihre Schaufeln und Harken / benutzen

_____

5. sie / den ganzen Tag / im Park / verbringen

   _____

6. Monikas Vater und Karls Onkel / die jungen Leute / begleiten

   _____

7. niemand / wollen / das Ereignis / verpassen

   _____

Freizeit (Leisure time)

- Many Germans enjoy working in their gardens. For those people who do not have a garden, there is a German institution known as the **Kleingärten** or **Schrebergärten.** This is a small plot of land within a large common garden that is rented to a person for growing flowers, fruits, or vegetables. These common garden areas might be within or on the outskirts of the city. Renters usually build sheds on their plots of land in which to store their garden tools.
- Many people in Germany enjoy organizing and joining clubs. This German institution is known as the **Verein** (*club*). Sports clubs are very popular, but there are clubs for almost every interest, such as stamp collecting, gardening, conversing in a foreign language, dog breeding, and cooking. Hundreds of thousands of these clubs exist in Germany, each one officially registered and with its own constitution and by-laws. Members pay dues and nonmembers are sometimes allowed to participate in events for a fee.

G. Die auch. Say that the people indicated also do these things.

Beispiel   Johann begrüßt den Lehrer. (ich)
       ➤ Ich begrüße den Lehrer auch.

Nützliche Wörter

alles *everything*

die Lage *situation* (pl. **die Lagen**)

das Werkzeug *tool* (pl. **die Werkzeuge**)

1. Ich vergesse alles. (Birgit)

   _____

2. Diese jungen Leute verschwenden ihr Geld. (du)

_____

3. Wir bestellen eine Pizza. (ich)

_____

4. Ihr seht schön aus. (du)

_____

5. Der Bus kommt und wir steigen ein. (ihr)

_____

6. Sie besprechen die Lage. (er)

_____

7. Wir erledigen die wichtigen Sachen. (du)

_____

8. Ihr nehmt die Werkzeuge mit. (du)

_____

III. Negative and Indefinite Words

■ Study the following pairs of indefinite words and their corresponding negatives:

indefinite	negative
ein *a;* **einige** *some*	**kein** *no*
etwas *something*	**nichts** *nothing*
jemand *someone, somebody*	**niemand** *no one, nobody*
immer *always;* **manchmal** *sometimes;* **oft** *often*	**nie, niemals** *never*
auch *also*	**auch nicht** *neither, not either*

■ Some other useful adverbs of quantity:

viel *a lot*

wenig *little, not much*

zu viel *too much*

H. Johann ärgert sich. *(Johann is annoyed.)* Complete the following sentences by adding the German equivalent of the English words in parentheses.

Mensch ärgere dich nicht

ärgern *to annoy*	**ruhig** *calm*
fröhlich *cheerful*	**schreien** *to scream, shout*
klagen *to complain*	**vertragen** *to bear, stand*

---

1. _____ ärgert Johann. (*someone*)

2. Aber Johann sagt _____. (*nothing*)

3. Er klagt _____. (*never*)

4. Johann bleibt _____ ruhig. (*always*)

5. Er ist _____ fröhlich. (*also*)

6. Aber Johann muß _____ tun. (*something*)

7. _____ kann das vertragen. (*no one*)

I. Ein Lehrer klagt. *(A teacher complains.)* Herr Klaus is having a difficult time with his students this year. A colleague of his is trying to find out what's wrong. Herr Klaus answers him in each case with the corresponding negative word.

Beispiel Haben Sie einige gute Studenten?
➢ Nein, ich habe keine gute Studenten.

In der Schule

<u>auf</u>passen *to pay attention*

auswendig lernen *to learn by heart*

das Klassenzimmer *classroom* (pl. **die Klassenzimmer**)

schweigen *to be quiet, silent*

die Tafel *chalkboard* (pl. **die Tafeln**)

---

1. Machen die Studenten immer ihre Hausaufgaben?

   _____

---

2. Passen die Studenten manchmal auf?

_____

3. Hilft jemand Ihnen?

_____

4. Schlagen die Studenten etwas vor?

_____

5. Schweigen die Studenten immer?

_____

6. Räumen die Studenten das Klassenzimmer manchmal auf?

_____

7. Putzt jemand die Tafeln?

_____

8. Lernen die Studenten etwas auswendig?

_____

J. **Beschäftigungen.** *(Activities.)* Select an element from each of the three columns to tell how much or how often these people do the activities. Write eight sentences. You may add modals such as **wollen** or **können** to some of the sentences, if you like.

ich	Schlittschuh laufen	niemals
meine Freunde	Ski laufen	oft
mein bester Freund	Rad fahren	viel
meine beste Freundin	Fußball spielen	zu viel
Mein Bruder/Meine Schwester	fernsehen	wenig
Mein Vetter/Meine Kusine	Geschenke bekommen	manchmal
Die anderen Studenten	um sieben Uhr	jeden Tag
Die jungen Leute	aufstehen	den ganzen Tag
Die kleinen Kinder	Musik hören	immer
Meine Familie	Briefe schreiben	jedes Wochenende
Die Nachbarn	mit seinen Freunden	
Der Lehrer/Die Lehrerin	zusammenkommen	

1. _____

2. _____

3. _____

4. _____

5. _____

6. _____

7. _____

8. _____

K. Und du? Answer the following questions in complete sentences.

1. Hilfst du oft deiner Mutter/deinem Vater? Wie?

   _____

2. Helfen die Studenten dem Lehrer/der Lehrerin? Wie?

   _____

3. Was tust du im Winter?

   _____

4. Wie fährst du zur Schule?

   _____

5. Hast du etwas Besonderes vor? Was? Kannst du es uns erklären?

   _____

L. Aufsatz. Write a paragraph of five to six sentences describing what you do during the day at home and at school. Where possible, use verbs that you have learned with separable and inseparable prefixes.

*Present Perfect with **haben**; Present Perfect of Modals; Present Perfect with **sein***

I. Present Perfect with *haben*

■ The present perfect tense consists of **haben** or **sein** followed by the past participle. The past participle of weak verbs consists of the prefix **ge-** + the stem + **-t**: **gemacht, gebummelt, gehört, gekauft**, etc. Weak verbs whose stem ends in **-d** or **-t** and verbs whose stem ends in **-n** preceded by a consonant add **-et** instead of **-t**: **geredet, geantwortct, gerechnet**. Study the present perfect of **kaufen**:

	singular	plural
first person	ich **habe gekauft**	wir **haben gekauft**
second person	du **hast gekauft**	ihr **habt gekauft**
third person	er/sie/es **hat gekauft**	sie/Sie **haben gekauft**

Notes:

1. In everyday German, the present perfect covers the meanings of the English present perfect and simple past: **ich habe gekauft** *I have bought* or *I bought*.

2. Verbs beginning with an inseparable prefix do not add **ge-** to form the past participle: **bestellt, erledigt, verbessert, zerstört**.

3. Verbs ending in the suffix **-ieren** do not add **ge-** to form the past participle: **gratuliert, studiert**.

4. Verbs with separable prefixes insert **-ge-** between the prefix and the stem: **aufgeräumt, ausgepackt, eingekauft, zugemacht**. The prefix is thus placed differently in the present than in the present perfect.

Ich mache die Tür <u>zu</u>.	*I close the door.*
Ich habe die Tür <u>zu</u>gemacht.	*I closed the door.*
Wir packen unsre Koffer <u>aus</u>.	*We're unpacking our suitcases.*
Wir haben unsre Koffer <u>aus</u>gepackt.	*We've unpacked our suitcases.*

5. In the present perfect, the past participle comes at the end of the sentence. All other material is inserted between the auxiliary verb (**haben**) and the past participle.

Ich habe Petra eingeladen.	*I invited Petra.*
Ich habe Petra gestern eingeladen.	*I invited Petra yesterday.*
Ich habe Petra gestern zu der Feier eingeladen.	*I invited Petra to the party yesterday.*

6. Strong verbs add **-en** instead of **-t** to form the past participle. Frequently they have a change in the vowel of the stem. Study the past participles of these strong verbs.

anfangen	angefangen	schlagen	geschlagen
beginnen	begonnen	schließen	geschlossen
beißen	gebissen	schneiden	geschnitten
binden	gebunden	schreiben	geschrieben
essen	gegessen	schreien	geschrien
einladen	eingeladen	schweigen	geschwiegen
finden	gefunden	sehen	gesehen
geben	gegeben	singen	gesungen
gießen	gegossen	sprechen	gesprochen
halten	gehalten	stehen	gestanden
helfen	geholfen	tragen	getragen
lassen	gelassen	trinken	getrunken
laufen	gelaufen	tun	getan
lesen	gelesen	vergessen	vergessen
nehmen	genommen	verlieren	verloren
rufen	gerufen	zerreißen	zerrissen
schlafen	geschlafen		

■ Some verbs have a vowel change in the stem, but form the past participle with the ending **-t**.

brennen	gebrannt	haben	gehabt
bringen	gebracht	wissen	gewußt
denken	gedacht		

■ The past participle of the above verbs is formed in the same way even when prefixes, either separable or inseparable, are added.

anrufen	angerufen
besprechen	besprochen
verlassen	verlassen

A. Eine Feier. *(A party.)* Rewrite the following story in the present perfect.

Beispiel   Britta feiert ihr Geburtstag.
   ➤ Britta hat ihr Geburtstag gefeiert.

Vokabular

backen (er **bäckt, gebacken**) *to bake*

decken *to cover; to set a table*

dekorieren *to decorate*

feiern *to celebrate*

der Gast *guest* (pl. **die Gäste**)

das Getränk *drink* (pl. **die Getränke**)

das Glas *glass* (pl. **die Gläser**)

der Kuchen *cake* (pl. **die Kuchen**)

der Saft *juice* (pl. **die Säfte**)

singen (**gesungen**) *to sing*

stellen *to put, place* (in an upright position)

warten auf + acc. *to wait for*

---

1. Sie lädt uns alle ein.

   _____

2. Wir helfen ihr.

   _____

3. Franz kauft Limonade und Saft.

   _____

4. Katja und Ute backen einen Kuchen.

   _____

5. Ich decke den Tisch.

   _____

6. Hans stellt die Gläser für die Getränke auf.

   _____

7. Wir dekorieren das Zimmer.

_____

8. Wir warten auf die Gäste.

_____

B. Die Feier. What did people do at the party? Create sentences in the present perfect out of each string of words and phrases to find out.

Beispiel   die Gäste / plaudern
      ➤ Die Gäste haben geplaudert.

1. Michael / seine Tonbänder bringen

_____

2. wir / die Musik auf den Tonbändern hören

_____

3. viele / tanzen

_____

4. wir / unsre beliebten Lieder singen

_____

5. Britta / uns aufnehmen

_____

6. wir / das Tonband hören

_____

7. wir / lachen

_____

8. wir / Kuchen essen und Limonade und Saft trinken

_____

C. Zuhause. *(At home.)* What did each of these members of the family do to help out at home today? Create a sentence from each string of words and phrases to find out.

Beispiel   Opa / alles einkaufen
        ➤ Opa hat alles eingekauft.

Zuhause

abtrocknen *to dry*	**der Rasen** *lawn*
aufhängen *to hang up* (er hängt auf, aufgehängt)	**reparieren** *to repair, fix*
	spülen *to wash, rinse*
das Bett *bed* (pl. **die Betten**)	**der Staub** *dust*
der Boden *floor*	**staubsaugen** *to vacuum*
fegen *to sweep*	**trocknen** *to dry*
das Geschirr *the dishes*	**wachsen** *to wax*
kehren *to sweep*	**die Wäsche** *laundry*
mähen *to mow*	**waschen** (er wäscht, gewaschen) *to wash*
Oma *Grandma*	
Opa *Grandpa*	**wischen** *to wipe*

Hausarbeit

die Hausarbeit machen *to do the housework*

die Fenster putzen *to clean the windows*

die Kleider aufhängen *to hang up the clothes*

den Rasen mähen *to mow the lawn*

die Wäsche waschen *to do the laundry*

den Boden kehren/fegen *to sweep the floor*

das Zimmer aufräumen *to clean, straighten up the room*

das Bett machen *to make the bed*

den Staub wischen *to dust*

das Geschirr spülen *to wash the dishes*

das Geschirr abtrocknen *to dry the dishes*

1. Lise / das Geschirr spülen

   _____

2. Hansi / das Geschirr abtrocknen

   _____

3. unsre Schwester Monika / die Betten machen

   _____

4. Vater / den Rasen mähen

   _____

5. Mutti / die Wäsche waschen

   _____

6. ich / den Boden kehren

   _____

7. Oma / die Kleider aufhängen

   _____

8. meine Brüder und ich / die Fenster putzen

   _____

D. Schon gemacht. *(Already done.)* Create conversations around the expressions given. The first person asks why the person named is not doing the chore mentioned. The other replies that the person has already done it.

Beispiel du / deinen Computer reparieren
➤ „Warum reparierst du deinen Computer nicht?"
„Ich habe meinen Computer schon repariert."

Im Garten

beschneiden *to prune, cut back*	**Unkraut jäten** *to weed*
die Rose *rose* (pl. **die Rosen**)	**das Unkraut** *weed* (pl. **Unkräuter**)
schon *already*	

---

1. Oma / die Blumen gießen

_____

_____

2. Elka / ihr Zimmer aufräumen

_____

_____

3. du / die Hausarbeit machen

_____

_____

4. Wolfgang / Unkraut jäten

_____

_____

5. Vater / den Rasen mähen

_____

_____

6. ihr / die Wäsche aufhängen

_____

_____

7. du / das Geschirr abtrocknen

_____

_____

8. deine Mutter / die Rosen beschneiden

_____

_____

II. Present Perfect of Modals

■ When modals are used with another verb, their infinitive is used as their past participle. In the present perfect, the modal follows the other verb.

Er hat mitgehen wollen.	_He wanted to go along._
Wir haben hier nicht bleiben sollen.	_We were not supposed to stay here._
Ich habe die Stadt nicht besichtigen können.	_I couldn't tour the city._
Die Kinder haben im Garten nicht spielen dürfen.	_The children were not allowed to play in the garden._
Du hast um zwei Uhr abfahren müssen.	_You had to leave at two o'clock._
Ihr habt die Zeitung nicht holen müssen.	_You didn't have to get the newspaper._

E. Was haben sie tun müssen? *(What did they have to do?)* Tell what each of these people had to do using the present perfect including an infinitive with the modal verb **müssen**.

Beispiel Lothar / das Auto putzen
➤ Lothar hat das Auto putzen müssen.

1. ich / den Boden wachsen

_____

2. wir / staubsaugen

_____

3. die Kinder / ihr Zimmer aufräumen

_____

4. die Rechtsanwältin / einen Brief schicken

_____

5. die Touristen / das Schloß besichtigen

_____

6. du / dein Bett machen

_____

Der Schwarzwald (The Black Forest)

- The legendary **Schwarzwald** (Black Forest) is in the state of Baden-Württemberg in southwestern Germany. Today, one sees typical straw-roofed farmhouses in the forest, and tourists enjoy using the trails for hiking and cross-country skiing. The main ways to enter the Black Forest are from the state capital Stuttgart to the east, Baden-Baden to the northwest, Freiburg at the center, and Basel, Switzerland, to the southwest.
- There are several resorts in the Baden-Württemberg region. Titisee has campgrounds and there are paddleboats and guided boat tours on Lake Titisee. The **Bodensee** (Lake Constance), at the meeting point of Germany, Switzerland, and Austria, is one of the largest lakes in Europe. The university city of Konstanz has public beaches that are filled with sunbathing tourists. Baden-Baden is a luxurious resort known for its curative mineral baths and spas.

F. Das darf man nicht. *(That's not allowed.)* The Schmitts are spending the day in a park, but they find that there are too many rules about what you can't do. They tell what they wanted to do, but weren't allowed to do. Use **nicht dürfen** in the present perfect to express the prohibitions.

Beispiel   Wir haben das Mittagessen zubereiten wollen.
➤ Aber wir haben das Mittagessen nicht zubereiten dürfen.

Im Park

der Baum *tree* (pl. **die Bäume**)

das Eichhörnchen *squirrel* (pl. **die Eichhörnchen**)

das Feuer *fire* (pl. **die Feuer**)

klettern *to climb;* **auf Bäume klettern** *to climb trees*

der See *lake* (pl. **die Seen**)

die Wiese *meadow* (pl. **die Wiesen**)

---

1. Wir haben im See schwimmen wollen.

   _____

2. Die Kinder haben Fußball spielen wollen.

   _____

3. Wir haben auf der Wiese essen wollen.

   _____

4. Unsre Tochter Birgit hat auf Bäume klettern wollen.

   _____

5. Vater hat angeln wollen.

   _____

6. Peter hat die Eichhörnchen füttern wollen.

   _____

G. Wollen ist nicht können. Two friends are discussing one of their vacations. Create conversations between the two about what the friend on vacation wanted to do and what he or she couldn't do. Use the activities in the illustrations.

Beispiel A: Wir haben segeln wollen.
B: Habt ihr gesegelt?
A: Nein, leider haben wir nicht segeln können.

1.

2.

3.

4.

5.

6.

7.

Auf Urlaub

angeln *to fish*	**surfen** *to go surfing*
reiten *to go horseback riding* (**geritten**)	**tauchen** *to go scuba diving*
rudern *to row*	**zelten** *to go camping*
sich sonnen *to sunbathe*	

1. _____

_____

_____

2. _____

_____

_____

3. _____

_____

_____

4. _____

_____

_____

5. _____

_____

_____

6. _____

_____

_____

7. _____

_____

_____

III. Present Perfect with *sein*

■ A relatively small group of German verbs, most of them expressing motion, forms the present perfect with **sein** as the auxiliary verb instead of **haben**. Here are some of the most common with their past participles:

fahren	er ist gefahren
fallen	er ist gefallen
fliegen	er ist geflogen
gehen	er ist gegangen
kommen	er ist gekommen
reisen	er ist gereist
schwimmen	er ist geschwommen

Other verbs that form the present perfect with **sein**:

<u>auf</u>stehen	er ist aufgestanden
<u>auf</u>wachen	er ist aufgewacht
bleiben	er ist geblieben
<u>ein</u>schlafen	er ist eingeschlafen
sein	er ist gewesen
sterben (er stirbt)	er ist gestorben
werden (du wirst, er wird)	er ist geworden

When a prefix is added to a verb that uses **sein** to form the present perfect tense, that verb usually also uses **sein** to form the present perfect tense.

<u>ab</u>reisen	er ist abgereist
<u>an</u>kommen	er ist angekommen
<u>weg</u>fahren	er ist weggefahren

H. Man fährt aufs Land. *(A trip to the country.)* A group of friends is going to spend a day in the country. Margarete tells how they set out. To find out what she says, rewrite the following sentences in the present perfect.

Beispiel Margarete wacht um sieben Uhr auf.
➢ Margarete ist um sieben Uhr aufgewacht.

Die Abfahrt (The departure)

ander *other*

bald *right away, immediately*

zu Fuß gehen *to walk, go on foot*

---

1. Sie steht bald auf.

   _____

2. Sie geht zu Fuß zum Bahnhof.

   _____

3. Lothar und Hans fahren mit dem Bus.

   _____

4. Die anderen jungen Leute fahren mit der U-Bahn.

   _____

5. Sie kommen um acht Uhr am Bahnhof zusammen.

   _____

6. Der Zug kommt um Viertel nach acht an.

   _____

7. Sie fahren um acht Uhr zwanzig ab.

   _____

8. Der Zug kommt um neun Uhr zehn an.

   _____

I. **Wo sind sie?** Use **gerade** (*just*) and the present perfect of the verb in parentheses to answer the questions about where these people are.

Beispiel Wo ist Marie? (weggehen)
  ➤ Sie ist gerade weggegangen.

1. Wo sind die Kinder? (zurückkommen)

   _____

2. Wo ist Onkel Wilhelm? (abreisen)

   _____

3. Wo ist der Lehrer? (mitgehen)

   _____

➢➢➢➢➢

4. Wo sind die Touristen? (wegfahren)

_____

5. Wo sind unsre Freunde? (ankommen)

_____

6. Wo sind die Studenten? (abfahren)

_____

7. Wo ist das Baby? (einschlafen)

_____

8. Wo ist Opa? (aufwachen)

_____

J. **Ein typischer Tag.** What did Christine do yesterday? Form sentences in the present perfect from the elements given to tell the story of Christine's day. Note that both **haben** and **sein** verbs are in the exercise.

Beispiel   um sieben Uhr / aufwachen
       ➤ Sie ist um sieben Uhr aufgewacht.

1. um sieben Uhr zehn / aufstehen

_____

2. gut schlafen

_____

3. zum Tisch / gehen

_____

4. Brot essen

_____

5. Orangensaft trinken

_____

6. zu ihrer Freundin Sara / gehen

_____

7. Die zwei Mädchen / zur Schule / zu Fuß gehen

_____

8. sie / ihre Hausaufgaben besprechen

_____

9. Christine / um vier Uhr / nach Hause / zurückgehen

_____

10. die Hausaufgaben machen

_____

11. mit ihrem Bruder / fernsehen

_____

12. um elf Uhr / einschlafen

_____

K. Und du? Tell what you and/or your friends and family did at the times given. Write a complete sentence in the present perfect in each case including the time phrase given.

1. gestern

_____

2. letzten Samstag

_____

3. letzten Sommer

_____

4. vor einer Woche

_____

5. vor einem Jahr

_____

L. Aufsatz. Write a composition of six or seven sentences telling what you and your friends (or family) did last weekend.

Commands: *du, ihr, Sie, wir*

I. Commands: *du*

■ To give a command to one person you address as **du,** you use the present tense **du** form minus the ending **-st.** Note that commands are written with an exclamation point in German.

Komm mit!	*Come along!*
Mach deine Hausaufgaben!	*Do your homework!*
Ruf ihn nicht an!	*Don't call him!*
Arbeite nicht heute!	*Don't work today!*
Öffne nicht das Fenster!	*Don't open the window!*

Most strong verbs that have the vowel change **e > i or e > ie** in the **du** form of the present tense have this change in the imperative as well.

Iß das Gemüse, Fritz!	*Eat the vegetables, Fritz!*
Lies diesen Artikel!	*Read this article!*
Sprich mit mir Deutsch!	*Speak German with me!*

Verbs whose infinitives end in **-ern** and **-eln** form the imperative in **-re** and **-le,** respectively:

Lächle!	*Smile!*
Rudre!	*Row!*

Haben, sein, and **werden** have irregular imperative forms for **du.**

Hab kein Heimweh!	*Don't be homesick!*
Sie fleißig!	*Be diligent!*
Werd(e) nicht faul!	*Don't become lazy!*

A. Die Ratschläge von Mutti. *(Advice from Mom.)* Little Georg is starting first grade. What advice does his mother give him? Use the **du** form of the imperative of the phrases given to see what she tells him.

Beispiel   nicht zu spät kommen
➢ Komm nicht zu spät!

Gute Ratschläge geben (Giving good advice)

artig *good, well-behaved* (said of children)

das Comicbuch *comic book* (pl. **die Comicbücher**)

etwas auf den Boden werfen *to throw something on the floor*

der Fehler *mistake* (pl. **die Fehler**)

kauen *to chew*

der Kaugummi *chewing gum*

leserlich *legible, legibly*

der Name *name* (pl. **die Namen**)

der Schreibtisch *desk* (pl. **die Schreibtische**)

werfen (**er wirft, geworfen**) *to throw*

<u>zu</u>**hören** (+ dative) *to listen, pay attention to*

---

1. dem Lehrer zuhören

   _____

2. artig sein

   _____

3. keinen Kaugummi kauen

   _____

4. nichts auf den Boden werfen

   _____

5. deinen Namen leserlich schreiben

   _____

6. keine Comicbücher lesen

   _____

➢➢➢➢➢

7. deinen Schreibtisch aufräumen

_____

8. mit den anderen Kindern nicht plaudern

_____

B. Jawohl! Use the **du** form of the imperative to offer your friend the things he or she is interested in.

Beispiel   Du hast Bonbons! Darf ich einige essen?
      ➤ Ja, iß sie.

Zwischen guten Freunden (Between good friends)

der Aufsatz _composition_ (pl. **die Aufsätze**)

die Flasche _bottle_ (pl. **die Flaschen**)

korrigieren _to correct_

das Paket _package_ (pl. **die Pakete**)

die Post _mail_

---

1. Du hast eine neue deutsche Zeitschrift! Darf ich sie lesen?

_____

2. Du hast einen Brief von Markus bekommen. Darf ich ihn öffnen?

_____

3. Alle haben Durst. Soll ich die Flaschen Limonade holen?

_____

4. Dein Aufsatz hat Fehler. Soll ich sie korrigieren?

_____

5. Die Post ist angekommen. Soll ich sie dir bringen?

_____

6. Wir haben Hunger. Soll ich eine Pizza bestellen?

_____

7. Du trägst viele Sachen. Soll ich dir mit den Paketen helfen?

_____

8. Du brauchst mein Buch. Soll ich dir das Buch geben?

_____

C. Reisepläne machen. *(Making plans for a trip.)* Veronika is helping her friend Friedrich make plans for a trip to Austria. Rewrite these sentences as familiar commands to find out what she suggests to him.

Beispiel   Du mußt genaue Pläne machen.
  ➤ Mach genaue Pläne!

Für die Reise

danach *afterwards*

dann *then*

genau *precise*

der Kaufmann *businessman* (pl. **die Kaufleute**)

das Reisebüro *travel agency* (pl. **die Reisebüros**)

der Angestellte vom Reisebüro *travel agent*
  (pl. **die Angestellten vom Reisebüro**)

der Reiseführer *guidebook*

die Reiseroute *itinerary* (pl. **die Reiserouten**)

sofort *immediately*

das Stadtzentrum *downtown* (pl. **die Stadtzentren**)

wählen *to choose*

zuletzt *finally*

1. Zuerst mußt du ins Stadtzentrum gehen.

_____

2. Du mußt eine Buchhandlung suchen.

_____

3. Du mußt einen Reiseführer kaufen.

_____

➤➤➤➤➤

4. Du mußt sofort nach Hause gehen.

_____

5. Dann mußt du den Reiseführer lesen.

_____

6. Dann mußt du eine Reiseroute wählen.

_____

7. Danach mußt du den Angestellten vom Reisebüro anrufen.

_____

8. Zuletzt mußt du die Koffer einpacken.

_____

II. Commands: *ihr*

■ To tell a group of people with whom you are on familiar terms to do something or not to do something, use the **ihr** form of the present tense without the pronoun **ihr**.

Kommt morgen!	*Come over tomorrow.*
Schweigt und macht die Hausaufgaben!	*Be quiet and do your homework.*
Ärgert den Hund nicht, Kinder!	*Don't annoy the dog, children.*

D. Die guten Schüler. A teacher gives advice to his class on the first day of school. Write what he says using the command forms for **ihr.**

Beispiel   die Kulis und Bleistifte nicht vergessen
       ➤ Vergeßt die Kulis und Bleistifte nicht!

> ## Die guten Schüler
>
> **gehorsam** *obedient, obediently*
>
> **das Klassenzimmer** *classroom*
>
> **der Lärm** *noise*
>
> **schmutzig** *dirty*
>
> **der Schüler** (pl. **die Schüler**), **die Schülerin** *student*
>
> **unterbrechen** (inseparable prefix) *to interrupt*
>
> **der Unterricht** *class, lesson*

1. ruhig sein

    _____

2. die Hausaufgaben nicht verlieren

    _____

3. dem Lehrer gehorsam folgen

    _____

4. die Übungen nicht zerreißen

    _____

5. im Unterricht nicht essen

    _____

6. keinen Lärm machen

    _____

7. das Klassenzimmer nicht schmutzig machen

    _____

8. den Lehrer nicht unterbrechen

    _____

E. Am Campingplatz. *(At the campground.)* The scout leader gives his troop instructions on how to set up camp. Write what he says using the command form for **ihr.**

Beispiel   die Schlafsäcke bringen
➢ Bringt die Schlafsäcke!

Am Campingplatz

anzünden *to light, kindle*

aufbauen *to set up (a tent)*

das Brennholz *firewood*

die Dose *can*

das Essen *food*

sammeln *to gather*

der Schlafsack *sleeping bag*
   (pl. **die Schlafsäcke**)

setzen *to place, put*

das Streichholz *match*
   (pl. **die Streichhölzer**)

der Topf *pot* (pl. **die Töpfe**)

das Zelt *tent* (pl. **die Zelte**)

zubereiten *to prepare*

---

1. die Zelte aufbauen

   _____

2. Brennholz sammeln

   _____

3. ein Streichholz anzünden

   _____

4. ein Feuer machen

   _____

5. die Dosen öffnen

   _____

6. die Töpfe auf das Feuer setzen

   _____

7. das Essen zubereiten

   _____

8. Wasser holen

   _____

III. Formal Commands

■ To give commands to one or more people you address as **Sie,** you use the **Sie** form of the verb followed by the pronoun **Sie.**

Steigen Sie bitte ein!	*Please get on board.*
Wechseln Sie hier das Geld!	*Change your money here.*
Trinken Sie dieses Wasser nicht!	*Don't drink this water.*

F. Ausbildungskurs. *(Training program.)* The teacher of a training program for young engineers gives his group instructions. Write the phrases below as **Sie** commands to find out what he tells them to do.

Beispiel   um acht Uhr kommen
        ➤ Kommen Sie um acht Uhr!

Im Unterricht

<u>au</u>stauschen *to exchange*

Fragen stellen *to ask questions*

der Gedanke *thought* (pl. **die Gedanken**)

die Idee *idea* (pl. **die Ideen**)

Platz nehmen *to take a seat*

---

1. einen Taschenrechner bringen

    _____

2. sich im Büro Nummer zwölf treffen

    _____

3. Platz nehmen

    _____

4. die Hefte öffnen

    _____

5. dem Lehrer zuhören

    _____

➤➤➤➤➤

6. Fragen stellen

_____

7. die Ideen besprechen

_____

8. Ihre Gedanken austauschen

_____

G. Du bist die Reiseleiter(in). *(You're the tour guide.)* Show a friend's grandfather around Hamburg. Give him a tour and some suggestions using the **Sie** command.

Beispiel   mitkommen
➤ Kommen Sie mit!

Fremdenverkehr (Tourism)

das Andenken *souvenir* (pl. **die Andenken**)

die Eintrittskarte *ticket* (pl. **die Eintrittskarten**)

das Foto *photo, picture* (pl. **die Fotos**)

Fotos machen *to take pictures*

die Kirche *church* (pl. **die Kirchen**)

lösen: Eintrittskarten lösen *to buy tickets*

das Viertel *neighborhood* (pl. **die Viertel**)

---

1. dieses Viertel besichtigen

_____

2. einen Reiseführer kaufen

_____

3. diese alte Kirche anschauen

_____

4. Eintrittskarten für das Theater lösen

_____

5. das Museum besuchen

_____

6. viele Fotos machen

_____

7. Geschenke in den Kaufhäusern suchen

_____

8. von dem Besuch ein Andenken mitnehmen

_____

Fremdenverkehr und Reiseandenken (Tourism and souvenirs)

- Between Würzburg, southeast of Frankfurt-am-Main, and Füssen, in the foothills of the Alps on the southern German border, is the **Romantische Straße** (Romantic Road). This beautiful area of castles, churches, and walled medieval cities is one of the most visited places in Germany. Along this route to the south is Rothenburg ob der Tauber, a completely preserved walled medieval city, which is one of the most popular tourist spots in Germany. Most of the buildings in the old city date from the 13th to the 16th centuries.
- Tourists in Germany often purchase souvenirs from the vast array of typical handicrafts, such as Black Forest cuckoo clocks, Hummel figurines, Christmas decorations from Nürnberg, toys made of wood from Seiffen, **Marzipan** from Lübeck, Bavarian **Lederhosen** (leather shorts), **Janker** Alpine jackets, and Dirndl dresses and skirts.

IV. Commands: *wir* "Let's do something"

- To say "let's do something" in German, use the **wir** form of the verb with the subject pronoun placed after the verb:

Fahren wir heim!	*Let's go home.*
Bleiben wir nicht hier!	*Let's not stay here.*
Suchen wir ein Taxi!	*Let's look for a taxi.*

H. Ein Tag auf dem Land. A group of friends is planning a day in the country. Reproduce their conversation by changing the sentences to commands with **wir**.

Beispiel   Wir sollen am Samstag aufs Land fahren.
➢ Fahren wir am Samstag aufs Land!

Auf dem Land

der Badeanzug *bathing suit* (pl. **die Badeanzüge**)	**der Rucksack** *day pack, backpack* (pl. **die Rucksäcke**)
benutzen *to use*	**der See** *lake* (pl. **die Seen**)
durch *through*	**der Wald** *woods* (pl. **die Wälder**)

---

1. Wir können mit dem Zug fahren.

   _____

2. Wir müssen die Fahrräder mitnehmen.

   _____

3. Wir sollen Brot und Käse kaufen.

   _____

4. Wir sollen die Rucksäcke benutzen.

   _____

5. Wir müssen die Badeanzüge einpacken.

   _____

6. Wir können in dem kleinen See schwimmen.

   _____

7. Wir können Fußball spielen.

   _____

8. Wir sollen durch den Wald wandern.

   _____

I. **Pläne für Samstag.** A group of friends is throwing out ideas about what to do this weekend. Express their suggestions using the command for **wir.**

Beispiel ins Kino gehen
        ➤ Gehen wir ins Kino!

1. ins Kino nicht gehen

   _____

2. den Tag im Park verbringen

   _____

3. auf dem See rudern

   _____

4. Hedda besuchen

   _____

5. Eintrittskarten für das Konzert kaufen

   _____

6. radfahren

   _____

7. zum Zoo fahren

   _____

8. in der Zooimbißstube essen

   _____

J. **Und du?** Write out three pieces of advice you would give to a new student. Use the command form for **du** in each case.

   _____

   _____

   _____

➤➤➤➤➤

Now write out three different suggestions you would give to two new students. Use the command form for **ihr** in each case.

_____

_____

_____

Write out three suggestions for your teacher using the **Sie** command.

_____

_____

_____

K. Aufsatz. Using the **wir** command and other command forms where possible, write a dialogue between you and a friend about what you are going to do this weekend.

Prepositions; Accusative/Dative Contrast with Prepositions (Two-way Prepositions)

I. Prepositions

■ Common prepositions in German are followed by either the dative or accusative case.

The following prepositions are always followed by the dative:

aus *out of, made of*

aus dem Haus gehen	*to leave the house*
aus der Stadt fahren	*to drive out of the city*
Das Gebäude ist aus Ziegeln.	*The building is made of brick.*
Der Pulli ist aus Wolle.	*The sweater is made of wool.*

außer *except*

Außer den Würsten haben wir alles gekauft.	*We bought everything, except for the sausages.*

gegenüber *across from, opposite*

Mein Büro ist gegenüber dem Rathaus.	*My office is opposite City Hall.*

mit *with*

Willst du mit mir einen Spaziergang machen?	*Do you want to go for a walk with me?*

nach *to; after*

Wir sind nach Österreich geflogen.	*We flew to Austria.*
Wann gehst du nach Hause?	*When are you going home?*
Wer kommt nach dir?	*Who comes after you?*
Ich habe ihn nach der Deutschstunde gesehen.	*I saw him after German class.*

seit *since*

Seit der Feier sind wir Freunde.	*Since the party we've been friends.*

von *from*

„Kommst du jetzt vom Stadtzentrum?"	*"Are you coming from downtown now?"*
„Ja, von den Kaufhäusern."	*"Yes, from the department stores."*

zu *to*

„Fahrt ihr jetzt zum Bahnhof?"   *"Are you going to the railroad station now?"*
„Nein, zum Flughafen."   *"No, to the airport."*

The following prepositions are always followed by the accusative:

bis *until, up to*

„Wie lange bleiben Sie hier?"   *"How long are you staying here?"*
„Bis nächsten Dienstag."   *"Until next Tuesday."*

Note that **bis** often combines with other prepositions: **bis an, bis zu.**

„Wie weit muß ich fahren?"   *"How far do I have to travel?"*
„Bis an das Stadtzentrum."   *"Up to the center of town."*

durch *through*

„Bummeln wir durch die Stadt."   *"Let's take a walk through town."*
„Ja, gern. Gehen wir durch den Park."   *"Yes, gladly. Let's walk through the park."*

für *for*

„Ach, du hast ein Geschenk für mich."   *"Oh, you have a gift for me."*
„Was meinst du für dich? Es ist für deine Schwester."   *"What do you mean for you? It's for your sister."*

ohne *without*

„Heute ist es kalt. Ohne deinen Mantel kannst du nicht aus dem Haus gehen."   *"Today it's cold. You can't go out of the house without your coat."*

um *around*

„Es gibt einen Garten um dein Haus, nicht wahr?"   *"There's a garden around your house, isn't there?"*
„Ja, und einen Zaun um den Garten."   *"Yes, and a fence around the garden."*

A. Präpositionen. Translate each of the phrases given.

1. die Haltestelle

   from the stop   _____

   to the stop   _____

   up to (**bis zu**) the stop   _____

2. die Mensa

   through the cafeteria   _____

   up to (**bis zu**) the cafeteria   _____

   to the cafeteria   _____

3. die Feier

   after the party   _____

   until (**bis zu**) the party   _____

   since the party   _____

4. dein Bruder

   for your brother   _____

   without your brother   _____

   with your brother   _____

5. der Sportplatz

   across from the playing field   _____

   through the playing field   _____

   out of the playing field   _____

6. das Ereignis

   since the event   _____

   after the event   _____

   until (**bis zu**) the event   _____

7. das Haus

   around the house   _____

   up to (**bis in** + acc.) the house   _____

   across from the house   _____

8. der nächste Film

   until (**bis zu**) the next film   _____

   after the next film   _____

   except for the next film   _____

➤➤➤➤➤

9. der Flughafen

    around the airport _____

    through the airport _____

    from the airport _____

10. die Buchhandlung

    except for the bookstore _____

    around the bookstore _____

    to the bookstore _____

B. Mini-Erzählungen. Complete these mini-stories with the missing definite articles.

1. Wir fahren mit (a) _____ Bus. Der Bus fährt durch (b) _____ Stadt.

    Wir fahren bis zu (c) _____ letzten Haltestelle. Die letzte Haltestelle ist

    gegenüber (d) _____ Kino. Wir gehen zu (e) _____ Kino und lösen

    Eintrittskarten für (f) _____ nächsten Film.

2. Die Studenten sitzen in (a) _____ Mensa und essen. Gerhard ist

    ein neuer Student und er redet mit (b) _____ anderen Studenten.

    Sie reden bis zu (c) _____ Deutschstunde. Sie stehen auf und gehen

    zu (d) _____ Klassenzimmer. Der Lehrer wartet auf sie.

3. Johann und Marie wohnen gegenüber (a) _____ Fußballstadion.

    Um (b) _____ Stadion gibt es immer viele Autos und Busse.

    In (c) _____ Wohnung hört man den Lärm von (d) _____ Straße.

    Johann und Marie wollen eine neue Wohnung in (e) _____ Vororten

    suchen.

4. Heute wandern wir durch (a) _____ Wald. Wir gehen zu (b) _____

    kleinen See. Wir können ein Feuer machen und in (c) _____ Wald essen.

    Nach (d) _____ Mittagessen wollen wir in (e) _____ See schwimmen.

    Um (f) _____ See wachsen viele Bäume.

5. Wir haben ein Haus in (a) _____ Stadtmitte gesucht. Wir arbeiten

   in (b) _____ Stadtzentrum und wir wollen nicht mehr mit (c) _____

   Zug zu (d) _____ Büro fahren. Wir wollen zu Fuß zu (e) _____

   Arbeit gehen. Wir haben ein Haus gefunden, und wir haben viel Geld

   für (f) _____ Haus bezahlt.

6. Mein Freund Karl arbeitet hier um (a) _____ Ecke in (b) _____

   großen Kaufhaus. Er kommt um fünf Uhr aus (c) _____ Kaufhaus.

   Wir wollen in (d) _____ neuen chinesischen Restaurant essen.

   Das Restaurant ist hier in (e) _____ Viertel. Deshalb können wir

   zu Fuß gehen.

C. **Zu ergänzen.** Choose one of the two prepositions given in parentheses in each case to complete the following sentences.

1. Die Menschen stehen _____ den Kiosk. (um, gegenüber)

2. Wir kommen _____ dem Haus. (durch, aus)

3. Ich will nicht _____ ihn gehen. (ohne, mit)

4. _____ seinem Geburtstag haben wir ihn nicht gesehen. (Seit, Für)

5. Junge Leute spielen Fußball _____ der Jugendherberge. (gegenüber, um)

6. Wir gehen _____ die Kirche. (zu, durch)

7. Meine Krawatte ist nicht _____ meinem Koffer. (zu, in)

8. Wir haben sie _____ der Reise gesehen. (nach, bis)

II. Accusative/Dative Contrast with Prepositions (Two-way Prepositions)

■ The following prepositions are followed by the dative when they are used with verbs expressing position or location, but by the accusative when used with verbs expressing motion toward a point. These are called *two-way prepositions:*

an *at, on, against, to*	**über** *over, above*
auf *on*	**unter** *under, below*
hinter *behind*	**vor** *in front of*
in *in, into*	**zwischen** *between*
neben *near, next to*	

Compare the following pairs of sentences:

an

dative   Die Kinder sitzen an dem Fenster. *The children are sitting at the window.*

accusative   Wir fahren an den See. *We're traveling to the lake.*

auf

dative   Die Teller liegen auf dem Tisch. *The plates are on the table.*

accusative   Er legt die Teller auf den Tisch. *He places the plates on the table.*

hinter

dative   Mein Fahrrad steht hinter dem Zaun. *My bicycle is behind the fence.*

accusative   Wir sind hinter den Zaun gegangen. *We went behind the fence.*

in

dative   Wir sitzen in dem Kino. *We're sitting in the movie theater.*

accusative   Wir gehen in das Kino. *We're going to the movies.*

neben

dative   Er arbeitet neben mir. *He works next to me.*

accusative   Du kannst die Tonbänder neben die Stereoanlage stellen. *You can put the tapes next to the stereo.*

über

dative   Eine Fahne hängt über der Straße. *A flag hangs over the street.*

accusative   Wir gehen über die Straße. *We cross the street.*

unter

dative   Der Hund steht unter dem Tisch. *The dog is standing under the table.*

accusative   Der Hund ist unter den Tisch gelaufen. *The dog ran under the table.*

vor

dative   Wartet vor der Kirche! *Wait in front of the church.*

accusative   Fahrt nicht vor die Kirche! *Don't drive up in front of the church.*

zwischen

dative   Es gibt einen Garten zwischen den Häusern. *There's a garden between the houses.*

accusative   Du kannst mit deinem Fahrrad zwischen die Häuser fahren. *You can ride your bike between the houses.*

Notes:

1. Some verbs that are considered to express motion when used with these prepositions:

   an die Tafel schreiben *to write on the board*

   ein Bild an die Wand hängen *to hang a picture on the wall*

   die Flaschen in den Keller stellen *to put the bottles in the cellar*

2. The preposition **über** followed by the accusative can also mean *about, on the topic of.*

Was wißt ihr über den neuen Studenten?	*What do you know about the new student?*
Sie reden über die Lage im Land.	*They are talking about the situation in the country.*

3. The prepositions **an, auf,** and **in** may contract with **das** to form **ans, aufs,** and **ins.**

D. Zu ergänzen. Complete the following stories and dialogues with the correct form of the definite article.

Vokabular

der Berg *mountain* (pl. **die Berge**)

das Institut *institute* (pl. **die Institute**)

legen *to put in a reclining or horizontal position*

die Schublade *drawer* (pl. **die Schubladen**)

spazierengehen *to walk, take a walk*

die Spüle *sink* (pl. **die Spülen**)

stecken *to put inside of*

die Wand *wall* (pl. **die Wände**)

die Wissenschaft *science* (pl. **die Wissenschaften**)

---

1. Der Lehrer geht in (a) _____ Klassenzimmer. Er schreibt seinen Namen

   an (b) _____ Tafel. Er hängt Bilder an (c) _____ Wand, über

   (d) _____ Schreibtisch. Er steckt seine Bücher in (e) _____ Schublade

   von (f) _____ Schreibtisch. Er legt seine Zeitung auf (g) _____ Tisch.

2. Ich gehe in (a) _____ Küche. Auf (b) _____ Tisch stehen Gläser, und die Gläser sind nicht sauber. Ich stelle die Gläser in (c) _____ Spüle und ich spüle sie. Danach stelle ich die Gläser auf (d) _____ Tisch.

3. „Bitte sehr! Wie komme ich in (a) _____ Theater?"

   „Sie müssen über (b) _____ Brücke gehen."

   „Ist das Theater weit weg?"

   „Nein, es ist in (c) _____ ersten Straße nach (d) _____ Brücke."

4. Heute fahre ich in (a) _____ Stadt. Ich möchte in (b) _____ Kaufhaus gehen. Das Kaufhaus ist an (c) _____ Marktplatz, gegenüber (d) _____ Dom. Ich kann neben (e) _____ Kaufhaus parken.

5. Fahren wir zu (a) _____ Universität. Wir können auf (b) _____ Straße parken und zwischen (c) _____ Gebäuden spazierengehen. Willst du in (d) _____ Restaurant in (e) _____ Universität essen? Das Restaurant ist hinter (f) _____ Wissenschaftsinstitut.

6. Meine Familie verbringt den Sommer auf (a) _____ Land. Wir fahren im Juni auf (b) _____ Land. Wir haben ein kleines Haus neben (c) _____ Wald. Wir wandern oft durch (d) _____ Wald, und wir wandern auch über (e) _____ Berge. Um (f) _____ Haus ist ein schöner Garten. In (g) _____ Garten spielen wir. Wir können auch in (h) _____ Garten essen. Wir stellen einen Tisch an (i) _____ Wand von (j) _____ Haus und wir sitzen an (k) _____ Tisch und essen zu Mittag.

Die Wissenschaft (Science)

- Germany has produced some of the greatest scientists and inventors of all time. The 20th century saw a flourishing of great minds in many intellectual and artistic fields. Because of Hitler, many of those brilliant figures were forced to flee Germany. Others were unable to flee and were murdered by the Nazis.

- Johann Gutenberg, born in Mainz (1397/1400–1467/1468), is often credited with one of the most significant inventions in history—printing from moveable type. With his invention, Gutenberg revolutionized the development and transmission of culture. The rapid development of science in modern times would have been impossible without the rapid and efficient dissemination of information that the printing press provided.

- Chemist and physicist Robert Wilhelm Bunsen was born in Göttingen in 1811 and died in Heidelberg in 1899. He developed a method of gas analysis, discovered the elements cesium and rubidium, and invented laboratory equipment such as the Bunsen burner.

- Wilhelm Conrad Roentgen, the German physicist, was born in Lennep, Prussia, in 1845 and died in Munich in 1923. In 1895, he discovered the short-wave ray, also known as the Roentgen ray or X-Ray. For this discovery, he was given the first Nobel Prize awarded in physics in 1901.

- The German physicist Max Karl Ernst Ludwig Planck was born in Kiel in 1858 and died in Göttingen in 1947. He was a professor at the University of Berlin. For his development of quantum mechanics, he was awarded the Nobel Prize in 1918.

- In 1954, Max Born won the Nobel Prize for his work in quantum physics. He was born in Breslau in 1882 and died in Göttingen in 1970. He was head of the physics department at the University of Göttingen from 1921 to 1933, the year in which the Nazis forced him to leave Germany because he was Jewish. He became a British citizen and taught at Cambridge University and Edinburgh University.

- One of the most famous physicists of all time is Albert Einstein. He was born in Ulm in 1879, and became professor of physics at the Kaiser Wilhelm Institute in Berlin in 1914. In 1934, the Nazis revoked his citizenship and confiscated his property because he was Jewish. He fled to the United States where he became a citizen in 1940. He worked at the Institute for Advanced Study at Princeton. He received the Nobel Prize in physics for his work in quantum mechanics, theory of relativity, etc. in 1921. He died in Princeton in 1955. *Time* magazine named Einstein man of the century in 1999.

E. Gegensätze. *(Opposites.)* Answer each question using the preposition that means the opposite.

Beispiel   Kommt er ins Haus?
> ➤ Nein, er kommt aus dem Haus.

1. Schläft die Katze auf dem Tisch?

_____

2. Fährt er hinter das Haus?

_____

3. Kommst du mit dem neuen Studenten?

_____

4. Parkt ihr vor den Geschäften?

_____

5. Geht er aus der Wohnung?

_____

6. Gibt es einen Kiosk vor dem Park?

_____

F. Hannelores Zimmer. Look at the picture of Hannelore's room. Then describe the location of the objects indicated.

Beispiel   Schultasche / Stuhl
> ➤ Die Schultasche hängt / ist auf dem Stuhl.

Hannelores Zimmer

das Bild *picture* (pl. **die Bilder**)

das Bücherregal *bookcase* (pl. **die Bücherregale**)

der Kassettenrekorder *tape recorder* (pl. **die Kassettenrekorder**)

die Lampe *lamp* (pl. **die Lampen**)

das Papier *paper* (pl. **die Papiere**)

der Papierkorb *wastepaper basket* (pl. **die Papierkörbe**)

der Sessel *armchair* (pl. **die Sessel**)

der Stuhl *chair* (pl. **die Stühle**)

die Tür *door* (pl. **die Türen**)

1. Bleistifte / Schreibtisch

_____

2. Kassetten / Kassettenrekorder

_____

3. Fahrrad / Tür

_____

4. Lampe / Bett und Sessel

_____

5. Katze / Stuhl

_____

6. Papiere / Papierkorb

_____

7. Bild / Wand

_____

8. Zeitschriften / Boden

_____

G. Übersetzen Sie! *(Translate!)* Translate the following pairs of sentences into German.

1. a. This train goes into the city.

   _____

   b. The railway station is in the city.

   _____

2. a. Put (= **stellen**) the wastepaper basket under the desk.

   _____

   b. The dog likes to sleep under the bed.

   _____

3. a. Grandpa likes to sit against the wall.

   _____

   b. Put his chair against the wall.

   _____

4. a. Don't drive between those buses!

   _____

   b. The stop is between those buses.

   _____

5. a. You can sit next to me.

   _____

   b. You can put your schoolbag next to me.

   _____

H. Und du? Answer the following questions in complete sentences.

1. Wohin fährst du dieses Jahr? In eine Stadt oder auf das Land?

   _____

2. Was hast du an die Wände von deinem Zimmer gehängt?

   _____

3. Wie gehst du in die Schule?

   _____

4. Wer sitzt neben dir in der Deutschstunde?

   _____

5. Wo treffen sich die Studenten? Vor der Schule oder hinter der Schule?

   _____

I. Aufsatz. Describe your room, your house, or your classroom. Tell where objects are in relation to each other and where people put things (**stellen, stecken**).

CHAPTER 15

*Word Study: **Gehen** vs. **fahren;***
Wissen vs. kennen; Liegen vs. stehen;
Legen vs. stellen; Attitude Words

I. *Gehen* vs. *fahren*

■ German distinguishes *to go on foot* (**gehen**) from *to go by vehicle* (**fahren**).

Oma geht aus dem Haus.	*Grandma goes out of the house.*
Wann fahrt ihr nach Australien?	*When are you going to Australia?*

■ Remember that when two-way prepositions are used with these verbs, the accusative is almost always used, i.e., whenever the prepositions indicate movement from one location to another ("direction").

Die Kinder haben Hunger. **Sie gehen in die Küche.**	*The children are hungry.* *They are going into the kitchen.*
Dieses Jahr fahren wir in die Schweiz.	*We are going to Switzerland this year.*

■ **Gehen** and **fahren** are conjugated with **sein** in the present perfect tense.

Wir sind auf den Marktplatz gegangen.	*We went to the marketplace.*
Ich bin nach Berlin gefahren.	*I went to Berlin.*

However, when **fahren** has a direct object, it is conjugated with **haben** in the present perfect tense.

Hast du dieses Auto gefahren?	*Have you driven this car?*
Er hat mich nach Hause gefahren.	*He drove me home.*

A. Ein Tag in der Stadt. Complete the following sentences with the correct form of the present tense of **gehen** or **fahren.**

Beispiel Heute _____ wir in die Stadt.
➤ Heute gehen wir in die Stadt.

1. Wir _____ zum Bahnhof.

2. Wir _____ mit dem Zug.

3. Der Zug _____ um 9 Uhr 20 ab.

4. In der Stadt _____ wir in die Kaufhäuser.

5. Wir kaufen viel ein und _____ in ein japanisches Restaurant.

6. Nach dem Essen _____ wir durch den Park.

7. Von dem Park _____ wir mit dem Bus zum Bahnhof.

8. Um 4 Uhr 30 _____ wir heim.

Die Schweiz (Switzerland)

■ Switzerland is known for its breathtaking mountains and lakes, chocolates, cheeses, and miniature trains. Located in the Alps, it is bordered by Germany on the north, Austria on the east, Italy on the south, and France on the west. It is a diverse country ethnically and linguistically, with about 65 percent of the population speaking German, 20 percent French, 10 percent Italian, and 1 percent Romansch. Romansch is a Romance language that has its roots in the Latin spoken in Helvetia, a province of the Roman empire, which occupied the land we now call Switzerland. All four languages are official.

■ The Swiss Confederation, made up of 23 cantons, obtained its independence from the Holy Roman Empire with the Peace of Westphalia in 1648. The federal constitution of 1848 joined the cantons, allowing each one much local control.

■ Bern, the Swiss capital, is on the Aare River. Visitors enjoy walking around the picturesque medieval **Altstadt** (Old City), with its **Zytgloggeturm** (clock tower), beautiful fountains, and elegant shopping streets such as the **Marktgasse.** They can visit the interesting **Schweizerisches Alpines Museum** (*Alpine Swiss Museum*) and Albert Einstein's house.

■ German-speaking Zürich, on the Limmat River, is the largest city in Switzerland and an international banking and financial center. Of great interest to visitors are the **Schweizerisches Landesmuseum** (*Swiss National Museum*) and the **Großmünster** (*cathedral*) that became a symbol of the Reformation in Switzerland. Boat trips on Lake Zürich offer panoramic views.

B. **Tourismus in der Schweiz.** Lotte describes what her tour group did in Switzerland. Complete the following sentences with the correct form of the present perfect tense of **gehen** or **fahren.**

1. Letzten Winter _____ wir in die Schweiz _____.

2. Von unsrem Hotel in Zürich _____ wir um die ganze Stadt

_____.

➢➢➢➢➢

3. Ich _____ oft in die Geschäfte _____.

4. Meine Freundin Lise _____ zweimal ins Theater

_____.

5. Mit einem Bus _____ wir in die Berge _____.

6. Wir _____ in kleinen Städten ausgestiegen und in viel Geschäfte

_____.

7. Danach _____ wir nach Zürich zurück _____.

8. Und wir _____ mit dem Schnellzug nach Hause

_____.

II. *Wissen* vs. *kennen*

■ German has two words that translate English *to know:* **wissen** and **kennen.**
Wissen means *to know facts or information.*

Weißt du das Datum?	*Do you know the date?*
Ich weiß seinen Namen nicht.	*I don't know his name.*

Wissen, not **kennen,** is followed by clauses.

Weißt du, daß er kommt?	*Do you know that he's coming?*
Wißt ihr, wo er arbeitet?	*Do you know where he's working?*
Ich weiß nicht, wie er heißt.	*I don't know what his name is.*

■ **Kennen** means *to know* in the sense of *to be familiar* or *acquainted with.*
It is usually followed by a person or place.

Kennst du diesen jungen Kerl?	*Do you know this young fellow?*
Sie kennt die Schweiz gut.	*She knows Switzerland well.*

- **Wissen von** means *to know of*.

Wissen Sie von einem Hotel in der Schweiz?	*Do you know of a hotel in Switzerland?*

- **Können** is very often used with languages and school subjects.

Sie kann gut Deutsch.	*She speaks German well.*
Diese Studenten können Literatur.	*These students know literature.*

- Note the use of the adjective **bekannt** to mean *known* in the sense of *well-known*.

Er ist ein bekannter Schriftsteller.	*He is a famous writer.*

C. **Ein Neuer.** *(A newcomer.)* Complete the following sentences about a newcomer in town with the correct present tense form of **wissen** or **kennen,** as required.

1. _____ du den Mann dort?

2. Ich _____ ihn, aber ich _____ nicht, wie er heißt.

3. Was _____ du von ihm?

4. Ich _____, wo er arbeitet.

5. Ist er Ausländer? _____ er hier viele Menschen?

6. Ja, er ist Ausländer. Er _____ gut Französisch und Englisch.

7. Ich glaube, alle _____ ihn.

8. Ich möchte _____, wie er heißt.

D. **Was wissen Sie?** Complete the following conversations with the correct present tense forms of **wissen** or **kennen.**

1. „Bitte sehr, wo ist das Fußballstadion?"

   „Ich (a) _____ das nicht genau. Ich (b) _____ diese Stadt

   nicht sehr gut. Ich komme aus dem Ausland."

2. „Wer ist dieser Junge?"

   „Ich (a) _____ nicht. Ich (b) _____ den Jungen nicht."

   „Fragen wir Christine! Sie (c) _____ alle Studenten. Christine!"

   „Ja?"

   „Wer ist dieser Junge?"

   „Ich (d) _____, er ist ein neuer Student. Aber seinen Namen

   (e) _____ ich nicht."

➣➣➣➣➣

3. „Du fährst nach Zürich. (a) _____ du jemand dort?"

„Nein, ich (b) _____ niemand in der Stadt."

„(c) _____ du? Ich habe eine Kusine in Zürich. Willst du ihre

Nummer? Meine Kusine (d) _____ Zürich gut."

„Aber ich (e) _____ wenig Deutsch."

„Das macht nichts. Sie (f) _____ gut Englisch."

III. *Liegen* vs. *stehen*

■ German usually uses **liegen** or **stehen** instead of **sein** to express the location of objects. **Liegen** is used to express the location of objects that are in a horizontal position.

Das Buch liegt auf dem Tisch.	*The book is (lying) on the table.*
Die Papiere liegen auf dem Boden.	*The papers are (lying) on the floor.*

The verb **stehen** is used to express the location of objects that are in a vertical position.

Die Flaschen stehen im Kühlschrank.	*The bottles are (standing) in the refrigerator.*
Mein Fahrrad steht vor dem Haus.	*My bicycle is (standing) in front of the house.*

■ Note the perfect forms:

Das Kind hat im Bett gelegen.	*The child was lying in bed.*
Wir haben vor der Schule gestanden.	*We were standing in front of the school.*

E. Beschreib! Describe the position of the objects in each of the following pictures. Use the present tense of **stehen** or **liegen**, as appropriate.

Beispiel Der Tisch _steht in der Küche_ .

1. Die Flasche _____ .

2. Die Flasche _____ .

3. Die Lampe _____ .

4. Das Lineal _____ .

➤➤➤➤➤

5. Die Schaufel _____.

6. Die Schaufel _____.

7. Die Bücher _____.

8. Das Geld _____.

IV. *Legen* vs. *stellen*

- Just as German specifies horizontal vs. vertical position, it also distinguishes between placing objects in a horizontal vs. vertical position. English *put* is therefore **legen** when you put an object in a horizontal position, but **stellen** when you put an object in a vertical or upright position. **Legen** and **stellen** are followed by the accusative after two-way prepositions, and are used with **Wohin** rather than **Wo** in questions.

„Wohin hast du die Papiere gelegt?"	*"Where did you put the papers?"*
„Ich habe die Papiere auf den Stuhl gelegt."	*"I put the papers on the chair."*
„Wohin hast du die Flaschen gestellt?"	*"Where did you put the bottles?"*
„Ich habe die Flaschen auf den Tisch gestellt."	*"I put the bottles on the table."*

F. Man erklärt. Explain why objects are where they are by saying you put them there. Note the use of **wieso?** *how come?* in the questions.

Beispiel   Wieso steht der Papierkorb unter dem Tisch?
          ➤ Ich habe den Papierkorb unter den Tisch gestellt.

Legen und stellen

der Herd *cooking stove* (pl. **die Herde**)

das Laken *(bed)sheet* (pl. **die Laken**)

der Regenschirm *umbrella* (pl. **die Regenschirme**)

die Schachtel *box* (pl. **die Schachteln**)

der Schrank *closet, cupboard* (pl. **die Schränke**)

der Teppich *carpet, rug* (pl. **die Teppiche**)

der Wäscheschrank *linen closet* (pl. **die Wäscheschränke**)

---

1. Wieso stehen die Dosen im Schrank?

    _____

2. Wieso liegen die Bücher auf dem Sessel?

    _____

3. Wieso stehen die Töpfe auf dem Herd?

    _____

4. Wieso liegen die Kulis in der Schachtel?

    _____

➤➤➤➤➤

5. Wieso steht der Regenschirm neben der Tür?

_____

6. Wieso liegen die Laken im Wäscheschrank?

_____

7. Wieso steht das Auto vor dem Kino?

_____

8. Wieso liegt dieser Teppich auf dem Boden?

_____

G. Hausarbeit. Frau Biedermann is calling upon everyone in the family to help her get the housework done. Complete the commands she gives them with the appropriate forms of **legen** or **stellen** and the missing definite article.

Beispiel Hermann! _Stell_ das Auto vor _das_ Haus!

1. Hansi! _____ deine Bücher in _____ Bücherregal!

2. Birgit! _____ die Laken auf _____ Bett!

3. Opa! _____ den Regenschirm in _____ Ecke!

4. Oma! _____ die sauberen Gläser in _____ Schrank!

5. Margarete! _____ die Wäsche in _____ Wäscheschrank!

6. Hermann! _____ den Topf auf _____ Herd!

7. Fritz und Karl! _____ den Teppich auf _____ Dachboden!

8. Opa und Oma! _____ die Dosen auf _____ Tisch!

H. Auf Deutsch, bitte! Translate the following sentences into German. Each sentence will use one of the following verbs: **liegen, stehen, legen, stellen.**

1. They put the pencils into the box.

   _____

2. Let's put the bottles into the closet.

   _____

3. My car is across from the park.

   _____

4. You can put your bicycle under the bridge.

   _____

5. The luggage is behind the door.

   _____

6. The candy is in the box.

   _____

7. Markus, put the firewood in front of the tent.

   _____

8. She put the photos on the table.

   _____

V. Attitude Words

■ German has a number of words that are added to the sentence to show the speaker's attitude toward the information in the sentence. Here are the most important ones:

aber

> **Aber** expresses surprise at the unexpected:

> **Deine Wohnung ist aber groß!**   *My, your apartment is big!*

> **Dieser Sessel ist aber unbequem.**   *This armchair is uncomfortable, isn't it?*

auch

In yes/no questions, **auch** functions like a tag in English: *haven't you, didn't he, aren't we*.

Hat er auch das Brennholz gesammelt?	*He did gather the firewood, didn't he?*
Hast du auch die Kartoffeln gekocht?	*You cooked the potatoes, didn't you?*

In information questions, **auch** expresses resignation, like the English word *well*, meaning *what else can you expect*.

„Mir ist heiß."	*"I'm warm."*
„Warum hast du auch eine Jacke aus Wolle angezogen?"	*"Well, why did you put on a woolen jacket?"* (= What can you expect if you put on . . .)

In commands, **auch** lends the idea of *"Make sure to do this."*

Komm auch um zwei Uhr!	*Be sure to come at two o'clock.*
Leg auch die Zeitung auf den Tisch.	*Make sure to put the newspaper on the table.*

Auch before a noun can mean *even*.

Auch der Lehrer macht Fehler.	*Even the teacher makes mistakes.*

denn

Denn is used to soften the tone of questions.

Kannst du mir denn helfen?	*You can help me, can't you?*
Warum studiert er denn Japanisch?	*Tell me, why is he studying Japanese?*

doch

When stressed, **doch** contradicts what has just been said.

„Gestern hat es nicht geregnet."	*"It didn't rain yesterday."*
„Gestern hat es doch geregnet."	*"It did so rain yesterday."*

Doch can be used with commands to make them sound more urgent or to communicate the speaker's impatience.

Mach doch nicht so viel Lärm!	*Will you stop making so much noise?*

eigentlich

Eigentlich can be used like English *actually* to soften questions.

| **Wo arbeitet er eigentlich?** | *Where does he actually work?* |

mal

Mal is used to soften commands.

| **Zeig mir mal die Fotos!** | *Do show me the photos.* |

nur

Nur adds a note of warning to a negative command.

| **Iß nur nicht die Bonbons!** | *You'd better not eat the candy!* |

Nur makes an information question sound urgent.

| **Kinder! Was habt ihr hier nur gemacht?** | *Children! What have you done here?* |

wohl

Wohl expresses the idea of probability.

| **Dieses Fahrrad ist wohl zu teuer.** | *This bicycle is probably too expensive.* |

I. **Sich besser Ausdrücken.** *(Expressing yourself more clearly.)* Rewrite these sentences adding the appropriate attitude word to express the ideas indicated.

1. Zieh den Mantel an!

   a. Soften the command.

   _____

   b. Add the idea of "make sure to."

   _____

2. Um wieviel Uhr ist die Deutschstunde?

   a. Make the question sound urgent.

   _____

   b. Soften the question.

   _____

➢➢➢➢➢

3. Diese Stadt ist sehr schön.

    a. Add a note of surprise.

    _____

    b. Add a note of probability.

    _____

    c. Contradict someone who has just said the city is ugly.

    _____

4. Leih ihm nicht das Geld!

    a. Make the command sound like a warning.

    _____

    b. Make the command sound more urgent.

    _____

5. Warum bist du gegangen?

    a. Add the idea of "what can you expect."

    _____

    b. Make the question sound urgent.

    _____

    c. Soften the question.

    _____

J. Und du? Answer the following questions in complete sentences.

1. Kennst du viele Menschen in deiner Schule?

   _____

2. Was liegt auf deinem Schreibtisch?

   _____

3. Wo stehen deine Bücher?

   _____

4. Wohin legst du deine Schultasche zu Hause?

   _____

5. Wohin stellt man die Gläser in deinem Haus? Wohin legt man die Laken?

   _____

K. Aufsatz. Describe where things are put away in your house. Mention who puts them away. Describe where things are in your room, using **liegen** and **stehen.**

CHAPTER 16

Subordinate Clauses; Verbs with Separable Prefixes in Subordinate Clauses; Modals in Subordinate Clauses; The Conjunction **ob***; Questions as Subordinate Clauses*

I. Subordinate Clauses

- A subordinate clause is a sentence that is part of a larger sentence. For instance, in the sentence *I know that John works at the supermarket, John works at the supermarket* is the subordinate clause. Subordinate clauses are made part of larger sentences by a subordinating conjunction, in this case the word *that*. The sentence *I know* is called the main clause.

- In German, word order in subordinate clauses is different from word order in main clauses. Here are the two sentences that would make up the larger sentence:

Ich weiß. Johann arbeitet im Supermarkt.

Note what happens to the position of **arbeitet** when the sentences are combined, using the subordinating conjunction **daß**:

Ich weiß, daß Johann im Supermarkt arbeitet.

In German subordinate clauses, the verb comes in final, not second, position.

Some additional examples:

Ich glaube. Der Lehrer ist heute krank. >
   Ich glaube, daß der Lehrer heute krank ist.

Er sagt. Marie wohnt hier in der Nähe. >
   Er sagt, daß Marie hier in der Nähe wohnt.

Ich hoffe. Alle Studenten studieren zwei Sprachen. >
   Ich hoffe, daß alle Studenten zwei Sprachen studieren.

- In the present perfect tense, the auxiliary verb comes at the end of the sentence.

Ich glaube, daß er gerade gekommen ist.	*I believe he just came.*
Ich hoffe, daß sie Milch und Brot gekauft haben.	*I hope they bought milk and bread.*

- Note the distinction between **das** *the, that* (article and pronoun) and **daß** *that* (subordinating conjunction).

Note also that a subordinate clause is preceded by a comma in German.

■ Here are some verbs and expressions usually followed by subordinate clauses beginning with **daß**:

erwarten *to expect*	**sagen** *to say*
glauben *to believe*	**versprechen** (+ dative) *to promise*
hoffen *to hope*	**wissen** *to know*
meinen *to think, be of the opinion*	**wünschen** *to wish*

es freut mich, daß *I'm glad that*

es gefällt mir, daß *I'm pleased that*

es wundert mich, daß *I'm surprised that*

es ist möglich, daß *it's possible that*

es ist nötig/notwendig, daß *it's necessary that*

es ist unmöglich, daß *it's impossible that*

es ist verboten, daß *it's forbidden that*

A. Weißt du das? Here are some facts about Germany and Austria. Ask your friend if he or she knows them.

Beispiel   Wien ist die Hauptstadt von Österreich.
➤ Weißt du, daß Wien die Hauptstadt von Österreich ist?

Deutschland und Österreich

die Donau *Danube (River)*	**die Industrie** *industry* (pl. **die Industrien**)
der Einwohner *inhabitant* (pl. **die Einwohner**)	**das Land** *country; German state* (pl. **die Länder**)
das Eisen *iron*	**das Nahrungsmittel** *foodstuff*
erzeugen *to produce*	**der Stahl** *steel*
der Fluß *river* (pl. **die Flüsse**)	**ungefähr** *approximately*
die Geburtsstadt *native city*	**verschiedenartig** *various*
gliedern *to divide*	
Haupt- (prefix) *main*	
die Hauptstadt *capital* (pl. **die Hauptstädte**)	

---

1. Berlin ist die Hauptstadt von Deutschland.

   _____

2. Deutschland hat ungefähr achtzig Millionen Einwohner.

   _____

➤➤➤➤➤

3. Deutschland ist in sechzehn Länder gegliedert.

_____

4. Deutschland erzeugt verschiedenartige Nahrungsmittel.

_____

5. Salzburg ist Mozarts Geburtsstadt.

_____

6. Die Donau ist der Hauptfluß von Österreich.

_____

7. Österreich hat ungefähr acht Millionen Einwohner.

_____

8. In Österreich erzeugt man Eisen und Stahl.

_____

Österreich (Austria)

- Austria is a German-speaking country in south central Europe. Austria is a federal republic divided into nine **Bundesländer** (*provinces*), each one with its own legislature. The head of state is the president and the head of government is the chancellor. Austria is a member of the European Union.
- Austria's main industries are iron and steel, machinery, motor vehicles, electrical equipment, mining, paper, textiles, chemicals, and food. Industry is found predominantly in Vienna and Linz, on the Danube River, and in Graz, on the Mur River. Tourism is also very important, especially in the Alpine provinces of the south and west.
- Salzburg, nestled in the mountains a few miles from the German border, is the city where Wolfgang Amadeus Mozart was born in 1756. The annual summer festival (the **Salzburger Festspiele**) honoring this great composer began in 1920. **Mozarts Geburtshaus** (*Mozart's birthplace*) at Getreidegasse 9 is visited by thousands of tourists each year. Salzburg is a city of great charm with many palaces, churches, and heavenly **Konditoreien** (*pastry shops*).

B. In der Stadt. Answer the following questions about your city for a foreign friend. Use **mir scheint, daß** in your responses.

Beispiel Was baut man hier? (ein neues Gebäude)
> ➤ Mir scheint, daß man ein neues Gebäude baut.

1. Wann schließt man die Geschäfte? (um halb sieben)

   _____

2. Wohin fährt dieser Zug? (in die Vororte)

   _____

3. Was gibt es hier? (der Markt)

   _____

4. Was erzeugt man in diesem Betrieb? (Maschinen)

   _____

5. Was verkauft man in diesem Laden? (Kleider und Schuhe)

   _____

6. Was für ein Restaurant ist das? (chinesisch)

   _____

7. Wo rudert man? (in dem Park)

   _____

8. Wohin führt diese Straße? (zur Universität)

   _____

II. Verbs with Separable Prefixes in Subordinate Clauses

■ In subordinate clauses, separable prefixes are attached to the verb in the present tense, as they are in the infinitive.

Das Kind schläft schon ein. > Ich glaube, daß das Kind schon einschläft.	*The child is now falling asleep.* *I think that the child is falling asleep now.*
Ich fahre heute weg. > Er glaubt, daß ich heute wegfahre.	*I'm leaving today.* *He believes that I'm leaving today.*

- Here are some other subordinating conjunctions that require verb-final word order:

als *when* (referring to a single event in the past)

bevor *before*

nachdem *after*

sobald *as soon as*

während *during*

weil *because*

wenn *when* (if in the present)

Ruf mich an, sobald du ankommst.   *Call me as soon as you arrive.*

Wir müssen die Reise besprechen, bevor du einpackst.   *We have to discuss the trip before you pack.*

- Subordinate clauses can also appear as the first element in the sentence. In this case, the verb of the main clause is the second element.

Als ich durch die Stadtmitte gegangen bin, habe ich Marie gesehen.   *As I was walking through downtown, I saw Marie.*

C. **Wir zelten.** Your friend has never camped and asks you questions about the routine when you camp out. Answer your friend's questions with the information in parentheses.

Beispiel   Wann sollen wir einpacken? (sobald / wir stehen auf)
      ➢ Sobald wir aufstehen.

Wir zelten

fertig *ready*

schlafen gehen *to go to bed*

das Zeltplatz *campsite* (pl. **die Zeltplätze**)

---

1. Wann fahrt ihr ab? (nachdem / wir packen das Essen und das Zelt ein)

   _____

2. Wann packt ihr das Auto aus? (sobald / wir kommen an)

   _____

3. Wann sammelt ihr Brennholz? (nachdem / wir bauen das Zelt auf)

   _____

4. Wann macht ihr Feuer? (sobald / wir finden die Streichhölzer)

   _____

5. Wann öffnet ihr die Dosen? (nachdem / wir stellen die Töpfe auf das Feuer)

_____

6. Wann esst ihr? (sobald / das Essen ist fertig)

_____

7. Wann könnt ihr plaudern? (während / wir essen)

_____

8. Wann geht ihr schlafen? (nachdem / wir räumen das Zeltplatz auf)

_____

D. **Jürgen und seine Mutter.** Jürgen's mother is giving him advice to make sure he gets everything done before his friends come over to watch a movie. Use the chart to write what she says. Each sentence will consist of a command from Jürgen's mother to him, a conjunction, and a subordinate clause. All the verbs in the subordinate clauses have separable prefixes.

Beispiel

command	conjunction	action
deinen Mantel anziehen	bevor	Du gehst heraus.

➤ Zieh deinen Mantel an bevor du herausgehst.

	command	conjunction	action
1.	deinen Mantel anziehen	bevor	Du nimmst den Müll heraus.
2.	Milch kaufen	wenn	Du kommst zurück.
3.	dein Zimmer aufräumen	bevor	Du rufst deine Freunde an.
4.	die Arbeit anfangen	nachdem	Du hast dein Zimmer aufgeräumt.
5.	die Hausaufgaben machen	während	Ich bereite das Essen zu.
6.	den Film aufnehmen	während	Du ißt zu Abend.
7.	deine Freunde einladen	nachdem	Du hast den Film aufgenommen.
8.	die Hausaufgaben fertigmachen	bevor	Deine Freunde kommen an.

Zuhause

der Abend _evening;_
    zu Abend essen _to eat dinner_

fertigmachen _to finish_

herausnehmen _to take out_

der Müll _garbage, trash_

---

1. _____

2. _____

3. _____

➤➤➤➤➤

4. _____

5. _____

6. _____

7. _____

8. _____

E. Im Restaurant mit einer Freundin. Roswitha tells about eating out with her friend Trudi. Join the sentences with the conjunction or expression indicated to find out what she says.

Beispiel   Ich gehe ins Restaurant. Ich ruf Trudi an. (bevor)
➤ Bevor ich ins Restaurant gehe, ruf ich Trudi an.

Im Restaurant	
bestellen *to order*	**Platz nehmen** *to take a seat*
der Kellner *waiter*	**die Speisekarte** *menu*

1. Ich esse in einem Restaurant. Ich gehe immer mit Trudi. (wenn)

_____

2. Es freut mich. Wir haben heute in einem italienischen Restaurant gegessen. (daß)

_____

3. Ich bin ins Restaurant gekommen. Ich habe Trudi getroffen. (als)

_____

4. Ich habe sie begrüßt. Wir nahmen Platz. (nachdem)

_____

5. Wir bestellen das Essen. Wir lesen die Speisekarte. (bevor)

_____

6. Ich habe ihr meine Fotos gezeigt. Wir haben auf das Essen gewartet. (während)

_____

7. Der Kellner hat die Suppe gebracht. Wir fingen an zu essen. (sobald)

_____

8. Wir haben gegessen. Der Kellner hat die Rechnung gebracht. (nachdem)

_____

F. Ursachen. *(Reasons.)* Use **weil** and the information given in parentheses to answer your friend's questions.

Beispiel Warum liegt Oma im Bett? (Sie ist müde.)
   ➤ Weil sie müde ist.

Probleme

bekommen *to get*

böse *angry;* **böse sein** + dative *to be angry with someone*

falsch verbunden sein *to have the wrong number*

die Grippe *flu*

naß *wet*

die Note *mark, grade* (pl. **die Noten**)

die Panne *flat tire*

pauken *to cram, study hard*

der Spaß *joke; fun* (pl. **die Späße**); **keinen Spaß verstehen**
   unable to take a joke

spät *late*

telefonisch *by phone*

---

1. Warum bist du nicht in der Schule gewesen? (Ich habe die Grippe bekommen.)

_____

2. Warum ist Mathias eine Stunde zu spät gekommen? (Er hat eine Panne gehabt.)

_____

3. Warum hast du eine schlechte Note bekommen? (Ich habe nicht gepaukt.)

_____

4. Warum hast du nicht mit Erika geredet? (Ich bin falsch verbunden gewesen.)

_____

➤➤➤➤➤

5. Warum habt ihr keine Deutschstunde gehabt? (Der Lehrer hat gefehlt.)

_____

6. Warum ist er dir böse? (Er versteht keinen Spaß.)

_____

7. Warum hat man eine Pizza gebracht? (Ich habe telefonisch eine Pizza bestellt.)

_____

8. Warum bist du so naß? (Ich habe meinen Regenschirm vergessen.)

_____

III. Modals in Subordinate Clauses; The Conjunction *ob*

■ Modals, like any other conjugated verb, stand at the end of a subordinate clause.

Er glaubt, daß er uns helfen muß.	*He thinks he has to help us.*
Sag mir, wann du kommen willst.	*Tell me when you want to come.*
Es freut mich, daß du kommen kannst.	*I'm glad you can come.*

Remember that when modals are used with another verb in the perfect tense, their infinitive is used as their past participle.

Ich habe nicht gehen dürfen.	*I was not allowed to go.*
Wir haben studieren sollen.	*We were supposed to study.*

When modals in the perfect tense appear in a subordinate clause, the auxiliary verb comes before the first infinitive and the modal verb comes at the end of the sentence.

Ich hoffe, daß sie gestern alle haben kommen können.	*I hope that they were all able to come yesterday.*
Weißt du, daß er nach Salzburg hat fahren müssen?	*Do you know that he had to go to Salzburg?*

■ The subordinating conjunction **ob** means *whether* (often *if* in everyday English). **Ob** turns a yes/no question into a subordinate clause.

Kommt er heute?	*Is he coming today?*
> **Ich weiß nicht, ob er heute kommt.**	*I don't know whether he's coming today.*
Kann er heute kommen?	*Can he come today?*
> **Ich weiß nicht, ob er heute kommen kann.**	*I don't know whether he can come today.*

Hat er heute kommen können?
> Ich weiß nicht, ob er heute hat
kommen können.

Was he able to come today?
I don't know whether he was able to come today.

G. **Ich glaube ja.** Some new students have questions about their new school. They answer each other's questions affirmatively using **ich glaube, daß . . .** + the modal in parentheses.

Beispiel   Fangen wir heute an? (sollen)
➤ Ich glaube, daß wir heute anfangen sollen.

Die neue Schule

<u>an</u>hören *to listen to*

freundlich *friendly, in a friendly manner*

Hausaufgaben <u>auf</u>geben *to give homework*

<u>zusammen</u>arbeiten *to collaborate, cooperate*

---

1. Arbeiten die Studenten gut zusammen? (wollen)

   _____

2. Geben die Lehrer viele Hausaufgaben auf? (müssen)

   _____

3. Tauschen alle ihre Ideen aus? (wollen)

   _____

4. Verstehen sie alles? (können)

   _____

5. Besprechen die Studenten ihre Arbeit mit den Lehrern? (dürfen)

   _____

6. Hören die Lehrer die Studenten freundlich an? (wollen)

   _____

7. Machen die Studenten viele Prüfungen? (müssen)

   _____

8. Kommen die Studenten nach dem Abendessen zusammen? (können)

   _____

H. Eine Feier im Zweifel. *(A party in doubt.)* Two friends are discussing the party that was planned. One asks questions; the other answers that he doesn't know whether the necessary things have been done. Write his answers using the expression indicated.

Beispiel Hat Marie den Kuchen backen können? (Ich weiß nicht, ob . . .)
➤ Ich weiß nicht, ob sie den Kuchen hat backen können.

Die Feier

die Ahnung *idea* (pl. die Ahnungen)   **sicher** *sure*

backen (**er bäckt, hat gebacken**) *to bake*   **zweifelhaft** *doubtful*

einsperren *to lock up*

---

1. Hat Lothar die Bonbons gekauft? (Es ist zweifelhaft, ob . . .)

   _____

2. Hat Kirstin den Tisch gedeckt? (Ich bin nicht sicher, ob . . .)

   _____

3. Hat man Erik eingeladen? (Ich habe keine Ahnung, ob . . .)

   _____

4. Haben Anna und Grete das Zimmer dekorieren können? (Ich bin nicht sicher, ob . . .)

   _____

5. Hat Veronika ihren Freund mitbringen wollen? (Ich weiß nicht, ob . . .)

   _____

6. Hat Werner etwas zu essen gemacht? (Es ist zweifelhaft, ob . . .)

   _____

7. Haben Joachim und Rolf die Katze im Keller eingesperrt? (Ich habe keine Ahnung, ob . . .)

   _____

8. Hat Karl die Gäste von der Haltestelle abgeholt? (Er hat mir nicht gesagt, ob . . .)

   _____

IV. Questions as Subordinate Clauses

- Information questions can also be incorporated into sentences as subordinate clauses. The question word functions as the subordinating conjunction, and the verb is placed at the end of the sentence.

Wo ist der Bahnhof?
> Ich weiß nicht, wo der
Bahnhof ist.

Where is the train station?
*I don't know where the train
station is.*

Um wieviel Uhr fährt der Zug ab?
> Du mußt fragen, um wieviel
Uhr der Zug abfährt.

What time does the train leave?
*You have to ask what time the train
leaves.*

Wo kann man in diesem Zug
zu Abend essen?
> Wissen Sie, wo man in diesem
Zug zu Abend essen kann?

*Where can one have dinner on this
train?*
*Do you know where one can have
dinner on this train?*

I. **Fremdenverkehr.** *(Tourism.)* Turn these questions into polite inquiries that you might use while touring Austria.

Beispiel Wie kommt man über die Donau? (Ich möchte wissen . . .)
> ➤ Ich möchte wissen, wie man über die Donau kommt.

Wien (Vienna)

die **Allee** *avenue* (pl. die **Alleen**)

aufführen *to perform*

das **Konzert** *concert*
(pl. die **Konzerte**)

kosten *to cost*

nachfragen *to inquire*

die **Oper** *opera* (pl. die **Opern**)

der **Pianist** *pianist*
(pl. die **Pianisten**)

der **Ring** *ring* (pl. die **Ringe**)

---

1. Wie kann ich zum Schönberg fahren? (Können Sie mir sagen . . .)

_____

2. Wann hat man dieses Gebäude gebaut? (Ich möchte wissen . . .)

_____

3. Welche Oper führt man diese Woche auf? (Wissen Sie . . .)

_____

4. Wie heißt diese Allee? (Sagen Sie mir, bitte . . .)

_____

5. Wohin führt diese Straße? (Können Sie mir sagen . . .)

_____

➤➤➤➤➤

6. Wie können wir zum Ring kommen? (Darf ich Sie fragen . . .)

_____

7. Wer ist der Pianist heute in dem Konzert? (Wir müssen nachfragen . . .)

_____

8. Wieviel kostet eine Eintrittskarte zum Konzert? (Sagen Sie mir, bitte . . .)

_____

J. Die Zukunft. _(The future.)_ Some students are discussing their plans for the future. Combine each pair of sentences into a single sentence to find out what they are thinking. Remember that a yes/no question is incorporated into a larger sentence by means of the conjunction **ob.**

Beispiel   Wann kann ich mein Studium abschließen? (Ich weiß nicht.)
➤ Ich weiß nicht, wann ich mein Studium abschließen kann.

Pläne für die Zukunft

<u>ab</u>schließen _to finish_

das Ausland _foreign country;_ im Ausland _abroad_

der Berufsberater _career counselor_

<u>ein</u>schlagen _to choose a career or course of study_

entscheiden _to decide_ (past participle **entschieden**)

die Informatik _computer science_

die Laufbahn _career_ (pl. **die Laufbahnen**)

der Rat _piece of advice_ (pl. **die Ratschläge**)

raten _to advise_

das Studium _studies, schooling_ (pl. **die Studien**)

---

1. Wo soll ich Arbeit suchen? (Ich bin nicht sicher.)

_____

2. An welcher Universität soll ich studieren? (Ich kann nicht entscheiden.)

_____

3. Wo gibt es einen guten Berufsberater? (Ich weiß nicht.)

_____

4. Welche Laufbahn will ich einschlagen? (Meine Eltern fragen mich immer.)

   _____

5. Was muß ich jetzt studieren? (Niemand kann mir sagen.)

   _____

6. Soll ich ein Jahr im Ausland arbeiten? (Kannst du mir raten?)

   _____

7. Muß man heute Informatik studieren? (Ich will wissen.)

   _____

8. Wer kann mir einen guten Rat geben? (Ich weiß nicht.)

   _____

K. **Und du?** Write your reactions to each of these ideas by adding a phrase such as **Es freut mich, daß . . . , Ich bin sicher, daß . . . , Ich kann nicht glauben, daß . . . , Es gefällt mir (nicht), daß . . . , Es ist nötig/ notwendig, daß . . . , Es ist möglich/unmöglich, daß . . .**

1. Unsre Lehrer geben viel Arbeit auf.

   _____

2. Wir müssen viele Prüfungen machen.

   _____

3. Die Eintrittskarten zum Kino sind sehr teuer.

   _____

4. Die Studenten in meiner Schule sind sehr nett.

   _____

5. Wir müssen viel Zeit in der Bibliothek verbringen.

   _____

L. **Aufsatz.** Write a dialogue between two friends about their plans for the weekend. Use as many subordinate clauses as possible.

Future Tense; Reflexive Verbs; Dative Reflexive Pronouns

I. Future Tense

■ The future tense in German is formed with the auxiliary verb **werden** followed by the infinitive.

	singular	plural
first person	ich werde gehen	wir werden gehen
second person	du wirst gehen	ihr werdet gehen
third person	er/sie/es wird gehen	sie/Sie werden gehen

■ The future tense is less common in German than in English. The present is preferred when another element of the sentence, such as an adverb like **morgen,** makes it clear that future time is meant.

Morgen gehen wir ins Kino.	*Tomorrow we're going to the movies.*
Nächste Woche feiert er sein Geburtstag.	*He'll celebrate his birthday next week.*

The future tense is used to express the future when no other element of the sentence makes it clear that future time is meant.

Ich verspreche dir, wir werden gewinnen.	*I promise you that we will win.*

Especially with words such as **wohl** *(probably)*, **vielleicht** *(maybe)*, and **wahrscheinlich** *(probably)*, the future tense expresses an assumption or supposition about the present.

Sie werden wohl nicht zu Hause sein.	*They're probably not at home.*
Das wird wohl der Bahnhof sein.	*That's probably the train station.*
Er wird wohl das Fahrrad reparieren können.	*He can probably repair the bicycle.*
Sie werden wahrscheinlich ankommen.	*They'll probably arrive.*

A. Dieses Wochenende. Tell what these students are doing this weekend using the future tense.

Beispiel   Anna / ins Theater gehen
➤ Anna wird ins Theater gehen.

1. Rolf / mit seinen Freunden ausgehen

_____

2. ich / das Wochenende mit meinem Vetter Karl verbringen

_____

3. Astrid und ihre Familie / auf das Land fahren

_____

4. wir / in einem deutschen Restaurant essen

_____

5. du / auf dem Campingplatz zelten

_____

6. Ingrid / radfahren

_____

7. ihr / einen Stadtbummel machen

_____

8. Günter und Hans / Samstag bei mir zu Abend essen

_____

B. Vielleicht. *(Maybe.)* Answer each of these questions using the information in parentheses as an assumption. Use the future tense and **wohl** to show that you are just supposing.

Beispiel Wo ist Margarete? (zu Hause)
➤ Sie wird wohl zu Hause sein.

Nützliche Wörter

<u>aus</u>gehen *to go out (on a date or for an evening of fun)*

<u>her</u>kommen *to come here*

das Fax *fax* (pl. **die Faxe**)

<u>ein</u>gehen *to arrive, be received* (letters, faxes, notices)

die Aufnahme *picture, photo* (pl. **die Aufnahmen**);
  Aufnahmen machen *to take pictures*

---

1. Ich habe meine Uhr nicht. Wie spät ist es? (drei Uhr)

   _____

2. Die Frau dort ist Ärztin. Wo arbeitet sie? (in einem Krankenhaus)

   _____

3. Ein Zug fährt ab. Wohin fährt er? (nach Stuttgart)

   _____

4. Wie kommen die Gäste her? (mit einem Taxi)

   _____

5. Bei wem geht das Fax ein? (bei Herrn Hoffmann)

   _____

6. Mit wem geht sie heute aus? (mit Klaus)

   _____

7. Wer macht Aufnahmen? (Lise)

   _____

8. Wann fährt dein Bruder nach Berlin? (in den nächsten Tagen)

   _____

Stuttgart

- Stuttgart, the capital of Baden-Württemberg in southern Germany, is on the Neckar River, which flows into the Rhine. This industrial city reflects Germany's enormous progress and prosperity since World War II. It is the home of Porsche, Mercedes-Benz, and several well-known high-tech companies. Visitors can see the birth of the German automobile industry in the Porsche Museum and the Gottlieb Daimler Museum (Mercedes-Benz). Gottlieb Daimler, born in Stuttgart in 1834, invented a high-velocity gasoline engine which was to be used in the automobile. Daimler's company merged with Carl Benz's in 1926. Daimler-Benz merged with the American Chrysler Corporation in 1998, creating Daimler-Chrysler, an automotive giant of global reach.
- The famous German philosopher Georg Wilhelm Friedrich Hegel was born in Stuttgart in 1770. Tourists can visit his birthplace, which is a museum. Also of interest are the **Staatsgalerie** (art museum) and the **Staatstheater,** the city's most famous theater.

II. Reflexive Verbs

- Reflexive verbs are verbs that are always accompanied by an object pronoun (either accusative or dative) that refers to the same person or thing as the subject. Some German reflexive verbs correspond to English reflexives such as *to hurt oneself,* but most correspond to intransitive verbs, verbs that have no object in English. Compare the forms of German **sich waschen** *to wash up.* The reflexive pronouns **mich, dich, sich, uns, euch, sich** are accusatives.

ich wasche mich	I wash up
du wäschst dich	you wash up
er/sie/es wäscht sich	he/she/it washes up
wir waschen uns	we wash up
ihr wascht euch	you wash up
sie/Sie waschen sich	they/you wash up

Study the reflexive verb **sich waschen** in the present perfect tense. All reflexives are conjugated with **haben** in the perfect.

	singular	plural
first person	ich habe mich gewaschen	wir haben uns gewaschen
second person	du hast dich gewaschen	ihr habt euch gewaschen
third person	er/sie/es hat sich gewaschen	sie/Sie haben sich gewaschen

C. Was Martina täglich macht. Discuss Martina's daily routine. Tell what Martina does each day to get ready for school and what she does when she comes home.

Beispiel sich duschen
      ➤ Sie duscht sich.

Was man täglich macht

sich abtrocknen *to dry oneself*

sich anziehen *to get dressed* (past participle **angezogen**)

sich ausruhen *to rest, relax*

sich ausziehen *to get undressed* (past participle **ausgezogen**)

sich beeilen *to hurry*

sich duschen *to take a shower*

sich kämmen *to comb one's hair*

sich rasieren *to shave*

sich auf morgen vorbereiten *to prepare for tomorrow*

sich zu Bett legen *to go to bed*

sich zu Tisch setzen *to sit down at the table*

---

1. sich abtrocknen   _____

2. sich kämmen   _____

3. sich anziehen   _____

4. sich zu Tisch setzen   _____

5. sich beeilen   _____

(Wenn sie nach Hause zurückgekommen ist)

6. sich ausruhen   _____

7. sich auf morgen vorbereiten   _____

8. sich ausziehen   _____

9. sich zu Bett legen   _____

D. Was Martina gestern gemacht hat. Now repeat exercise C by telling what Martina did yesterday. Use the present perfect tense.

Beispiel   sich duschen
     ➤ Sie hat sich geduscht.

1. sich abtrocknen   _____

2. sich kämmen   _____

3. sich anziehen   _____

4. sich zu Tisch setzen   _____

5. sich beeilen   _____

(Wenn sie nach Hause zurückgekommen ist)

6. sich ausruhen   _____

7. sich auf morgen vorbereiten   _____

8. sich ausziehen   _____

9. sich zu Bett legen   _____

III. Dative Reflexive Pronouns

■   Many verbs take a dative reflexive pronoun. This is especially common with reflexive verbs that have a direct object. The difference between dative and accusative reflexive pronouns shows up only in the **ich** and **du** forms. Study the conjugation of **sich die Hände waschen** in the present and perfect tenses.

present

Ich wasche mir die Hände.	I wash my hands.
Du wäschst dir die Hände.	You wash your hands.
Er/Sie/Es wäscht sich die Hände.	He/She washes his/her hands.
Wir waschen uns die Hände.	We wash our hands.
Ihr wascht euch die Hände.	You wash your hands.
Sie/Sie waschen sich die Hände.	They/You wash their/your hands.

perfect

Ich habe mir die Hände gewaschen.	I washed my hands.
Du hast dir die Hände gewaschen.	You washed your hands.
Er/Sie/Es hat sich die Hände gewaschen.	He/She washed his/her hands.
Wir haben uns die Hände gewaschen.	We washed our hands.
Ihr habt euch die Hände gewaschen.	You washed your hands.
Sie/Sie haben sich die Hände gewaschen.	They/You washed their/your hands.

Dative reflexives

sich den Arm brechen *to break one's arm* (past participle **gebrochen**)

sich die Haare kämmen *to comb one's hair*

sich das Knie prellen *to bruise one's knee*

sich die Zähne putzen *to brush one's teeth*

sich die Haare trocknen *to dry one's hair*

sich das Bein verletzen *to hurt one's leg*

sich den Knöchel verstauchen *to sprain one's ankle*

sich den Fuß vertreten *to twist one's ankle*
   (past participle **vertreten**)

sich die Haare waschen *to wash one's hair*

sich das Frühstück <u>zu</u>bereiten *to make one's breakfast*

Der menschliche Körper (The human body)

der Arm *arm* (pl. **die Arme**)

das Bein *leg* (pl. **die Beine**)

der Ellbogen *elbow* (pl. **die Ellbogen**)

der Finger *finger* (pl. **die Finger**)

der Fuß *foot* (pl. **die Füße**)

das Haar *a single hair* (pl. **die Haare**)

das Knie *knee* (pl. **die Knie**)

der Knöchel *ankle* (pl. **die Knöchel**)

der Knochen *bone* (pl. **die Knochen**)

der Körper *body* (pl. **die Körper**)

der Rücken *back* (pl. **die Rücken**)

der Zahn *tooth* (pl. **die Zähne**)

E. **Vormittags.** *(In the morning.)* What does Gretchen do to get ready to go out in the morning? Gretchen will tell you using the **ich** form of the verbs indicated. Be careful to distinguish between reflexive pronouns that are indirect objects and those that are direct objects.

Beispiel   sich die Hände waschen
   ➤ Ich wasche mir die Hände.

1. sich beeilen

2. sich die Zähne putzen

_____

3. sich die Haare waschen

_____

4. sich die Haare trocknen

_____

5. sich die Haare kämmen

_____

6. sich das Frühstück zubereiten

_____

7. sich zu Tisch setzen und essen

_____

8. sich den Mantel anziehen

_____

F. Gespräch zwischen einer Mutter und ihrem Sohn. Frau Strunk is telling her son Gustav what to do before he goes to bed. In each case, he tells her that he has already done that. Create the conversation between them using a command form in Frau Strunk's sentence and the perfect tense in Gustav's answer. Be careful to distinguish between reflexive pronouns that are indirect objects and those that are direct objects.

Beispiel   sich die Hände waschen
       ➤ Gustav, wasch dir die Hände!
         Ich habe mir schon die Hände gewaschen.

1. sich die Zähne putzen

_____

_____

2. sich rasieren

_____

_____

➤➤➤➤➤

3. sich die Haare waschen

_____

_____

4. sich die Haare kämmen

_____

_____

5. sich die Schuhe ausziehen

_____

_____

6. sich zu Bett legen

_____

_____

G. Warnungen. Now Frau Strunk gives Gustav advice about what not to do while he is playing in the soccer game. He answers in each case by telling her not to worry, and that he won't do these things.

Beispiel   Zieh dir das Hemd nicht aus!
➤ Keine Angst! Ich werde mir das Hemd nicht ausziehen.

1. sich den Fuß vertreten

_____

2. sich die Knie prellen

_____

3. sich die Beine verletzen

_____

4. sich den Arm brechen

_____

5. sich den Kopf verletzen

_____

H. Sie haben viel Spaß. *(They're having a lot of fun!)* Tell what kind of day three friends had last Saturday. Use the present perfect tense in each sentence. Note that many of the reflexive verbs used have either direct objects or prepositional objects.

Beispiel   die Jungen / sich für etwas Interessantes entscheiden
➤ Die Jungen haben sich für etwas Interessantes entschieden.

Verben für einen Tag mit viel Spaß

sich anhören (+ acc.) *to listen to*

sich ansehen (+ acc.) *to have a look at, watch*
(past participle **angesehen**)

sich ausdenken (+ acc.) *to think up* (past participle **ausgedacht**)

sich beschäftigen mit *to occupy oneself with*

sich entscheiden für *to decide to* (past participle **entschieden**)

sich entspannen *to relax*

sich langweilen *to be bored*

sich treffen *to meet* (past participle **getroffen**)

sich unterhalten *to chat, converse* (past participle **unterhalten**)

---

1. sie / einen Plan / sich ausdenken

   _____

2. Markus und Günter / bei Jakob / sich treffen

   _____

3. die Jungen / sich nicht langweilen

   _____

4. sie / die neuen CDs / sich anhören

   _____

5. sie / mit ihren Fahrrädern / sich beschäftigen

   _____

6. sie / einen Film / sich ansehen

   _____

7. sie / sich unterhalten

_____

8. die Jungen / sich gut entspannen

_____

I. Sie machen Pläne. Now talk about how the boys made their plans for spending the day at Jakob's house. Use the future tense in each sentence to listen in on their discussion.

Beispiel   wir / etwas Interessantes / sich einigen auf
➤ Wir werden uns auf etwas Interessantes einigen.

Pläne machen

sich einigen auf + acc. *to agree on*

sich konzentrieren auf + acc. *to concentrate on*

sich überlegen *to think about, reflect, consider*

---

1. wir / den Plan / sich überlegen

_____

2. wir / über den Tag / sich unterhalten

_____

3. wir / auf unsre Pläne / sich konzentrieren

_____

4. wir / bei Jakob / sich treffen

_____

5. wir / mit unsern Fahrrädern / sich beschäftigen

_____

6. wir / die neuen CDs / sich anhören

_____

7. wir / einen Film / sich ansehen

_____

8. wir / sich gut entspannen

_____

J. Mein Bruder. Gisela talks about her little brother. Compose sentences out of each string of words and phrases to find out what she says.

Beispiel   mein Bruder Hansi / sich gut benehmen
           ➤ Mein Bruder Hansi benimmt sich gut.

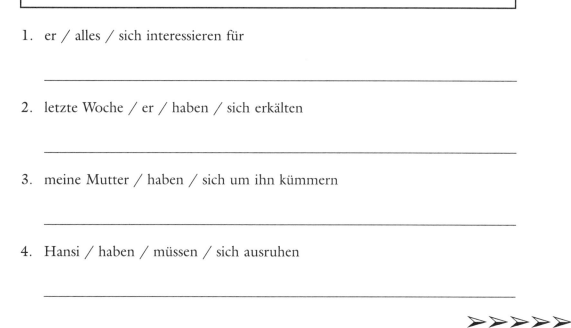

Gisela und ihr Bruder

sich (wohl) fühlen _to feel good_

sich ausruhen _to rest_

sich benehmen _to behave_

die Besserung _improvement, recovery_ (pl. **die Besserungen**)

sich erholen _to recover_

sich erkälten _to catch cold_

sich ernähren _to eat, nourish oneself_

sich freuen über + acc. _to be happy about_

sich interessieren für _to be interested in_

sich kümmern um _to take care of_

1. er / alles / sich interessieren für

_____

2. letzte Woche / er / haben / sich erkälten

_____

3. meine Mutter / haben / sich um ihn kümmern

_____

4. Hansi / haben / müssen / sich ausruhen

_____

➤➤➤➤➤

5. er / haben / gut / sich ernähren

_____

6. Hansi / haben / sich erholen

_____

7. jetzt / er / sich wohl fühlen

_____

8. er / über seine Besserung / sich freuen

_____

K. Eine Freundin beraten. Petra is concerned about her friend Renate, who is unhappy about her new job. Complete the story using the words and phrases given to find out how Petra helps her.

Beispiel   Meine Freundin Renate / haben / eine neue Stelle / sich bemühen
➤ Meine Freundin Renate hat sich um eine neue Stelle bemüht.

Arbeitsprobleme

sich bewerben (bei) _to apply (to)_

sich erinnern an + acc. _to remember_

sich erkundigen nach _to inquire about, ask about_

die Firma _firm, company_ (pl. **die Firmen**)

sich freuen auf + acc. _to look forward to_

sich gewöhnen an + acc. _to get used to_

raten _to advise_ (**er rät, er hat geraten**)

die Ruhe _rest, quiet;_ **in Ruhe** _calmly_

sehr _a lot_

sich sorgen um _to worry about_

die Stelle _job, position_ (pl. **die Stellen**)

sich überzeugen _to be convinced_

die Zukunft _future_

---

1. sie / haben / nach einer Stelle / sich erkundigen

   _____

2. sie / haben / bei einer Firma / sich bewerben

   _____

   Sie hat die Stelle bekommen!

3. sie / haben / auf die neue Stelle / sich freuen

   _____

4. sie / können / an die neue Stelle / sich nicht gewöhnen

   Aber _____

5. sie / um ihre Zukunft / sehr / sich sorgen

   _____

6. wir / haben / in einem Café / sich treffen

   _____

7. wir / haben / können / in Ruhe / sich unterhalten

   Da _____

8. du / müssen / sich entspannen

   _____ , habe ich zu ihr gesagt.

9. du / sollen / an die alte Stelle / sich erinnern

   _____ , habe ich ihr geraten.

10. sie / haben / sich überzeugen

    _____

11. sie / haben / bei mir / sich bedanken

    _____

12. sie / haben / sich beruhigen

    _____

L. Und du? Answer the following questions in complete sentences.

1. Wievielmal am Tag putzt du dir die Zähne?

   _____

2. Hast du dir schon einmal den Arm gebrochen oder die Knie geprellt oder den Knöchel verstaucht? Und deine Freunde?

   _____

3. Erinnerst du dich an deinen ersten Lehrer / an deine erste Lehrerin?

   _____

4. Was für Filme siehst du dir gern an?

   _____

5. Was für eine Musik hörst du dir gern an?

   _____

M. Aufsatz. Discuss the daily routine that you and your family have. Use as many rcflexive verbs as you can.

Relative Clauses; Relative Pronouns after Prepositions; The Narrative Past of **haben, sein,** *and the Modals*

I. Relative Clauses

- A relative clause modifies a noun the same way that an adjective does. Compare the following two phrases:

the new house
the house that we bought

The clause *that we bought* modifies *house* in the same way that the adjective *new* does. A relative clause is introduced by a relative pronoun. Compare the following two German sentences:

Wo ist die Frau, die hier arbeitet?	*Where is the woman who works here?*
Wo ist die Frau, die du kennst?	*Where is the woman whom you know?*

The relative pronoun is **die** in both cases because **die** refers to **Frau,** which is feminine and singular. Note that relative clauses have subordinate clause word order with the verb at the end of the sentence, and that a comma is required before the relative clause. Now compare these two sentences:

Wo ist der Mann, der hier arbeitet?	*Where is the man who works here?*
Wo ist der Mann, den du kennst?	*Where is the man whom you know?*

Note that the relative pronouns **der** and **den** are masculine singular because they both refer to **Mann,** but that **der** is nominative because it is the subject of its clause. The relative pronoun **den** is accusative because it is the direct object of the verb in its clause (**kennst**). Thus, the relative pronouns in German agree in gender and number with the noun in the main clause (the antecedent), but take their case from their function in the relative clause.

	masculine singular	feminine singular	neuter singular	plural
nominative	der	die	das	die
dative	dem	der	dem	denen
accusative	den	die	das	die

Note that the relative pronouns have the same forms as the definite articles except for the dative plural.

There are also genitive forms of the relative pronouns which are most frequent in the meaning *whose*.

	masculine singular	feminine singular	neuter singular	plural
genitive	dessen	deren	dessen	deren

■ Relative pronouns may be omitted in English, but NEVER in German.

das Buch, das ich gelesen habe   *the book (that) I read*

A. Um genauer zu beschreiben. *(To describe more precisely.)* Complete the description of these people and things with the appropriate relative pronoun.

Beispiel   der junge Ingenieur, <u> der </u> hier arbeitet

Nützliche Wörter

die Akte *file, record* (pl. **die Akten**)

die Aktentasche *briefcase* (pl. **die Aktentaschen**)

der/die Angestellte *employee* (pl. **die Angestellten**)

erreichen *to contact*

frei *free;* **einen freien Tag haben** *to have a day off*

das Gemälde *painting* (pl. **die Gemälde**)

der Künstler *artist* (pl. **die Künstler;** fem. **die Künstlerin**)

sich nähern + dat. *to approach, come close to*

offen *open*

der Pinsel *paintbrush* (pl. **die Pinsel**)

das Spielzeug *toy* (pl. **die Spielzeuge**)

---

1. a.   der Geschäftsmann, _____ wir erreicht haben

   b.   _____ wir einen Brief schreiben

   c.   _____ Büro wir besucht haben

   d.   _____ Nahrungsmittel verkauft

2. a.   die Rechtsanwältin, _____ Aktentasche auf dem Tisch liegt

   b.   _____ wir die Akten gegeben haben

   c.   _____ wir angerufen haben

   d.   _____ sich mit unserem Rechtsanwalt unterhalten hat

3. a.   der Künstler, _____ sehr berühmt ist

   b.   _____ alle bewundern

   c.   _____ dieser Pinsel gehört

   d.   _____ Gemälde wir gekauft haben

4. a. das Kind, _____ die Mutter böse ist

   b. _____ sich erkältet hat

   c. _____ wir besuchen

   d. _____ Mutter sich sehr sorgt

5. a. die Lehrerinnen, _____ viele Studenten haben

   b. _____ die Kinder gern haben

   c. _____ Klassenstunden interessant sind

   d. _____ wir helfen müssen

6. a. die Läden, _____ Angestellten sonntags einen freien Tag
      haben wollen

   b. _____ wir uns nähern

   c. _____ sonntags offen sind

   d. _____ du hier neben dem Kino siehst

Gesellschaft im Wandel (A changing society)

Retail store hours in Germany have been tightly restricted by law. Traditionally, German shops closed on weekdays by 6:30 P.M. and Saturdays by 2:00 P.M. A loosening of the laws allowed stores to remain open until 6:00 P.M. on the first Saturday of each month. Then stores were also permitted to remain open until 6:00 P.M. on the four Saturdays before Christmas. Thursday became a late night with stores remaining open until 8:30 P.M. Stores are now given more freedom to operate longer hours during the week. Traditionally, stores have been closed on legal holidays and all day Sunday, except for bakeries. Recently, 50,000 Berliners turned out to shop on a Sunday at a **Kaufhof** (department store) on the Alexanderplatz when the manager opened the store using a legal loophole. The following Sunday, 80,000 people turned out to shop there. It appears that before too long Sunday store closings will be a thing of the past.

B. Am Computer. Several office workers are discussing how they use their computers. Combine each pair of sentences into a single one using a relative clause to see what they say.

Beispiel   Das ist der Computer. Man hat mir diesen Computer gegeben.
➤ Das ist der Computer, den man mir gegeben hat.

Der Computer

ausdrucken *to print out*

ausschalten *to switch off*

bearbeiten *to edit*

das Betriebssystem *operating system* (pl. **die Betriebssysteme**)

der Bildschirm *screen* (pl. **die Bildschirme**)

die Datei *file* (pl. **die Dateien**)

drücken *to press;* **auf eine Taste drücken** *to press a key*

einschalten *to switch on*

einfügen *to paste*

die elektronische Post *e-mail*

das Ikon *icon* (pl. **die Ikonen**)

kopieren *to copy*

laden *to load* (**er lädt, hat geladen**)

die Maus *mouse* (pl. **die Mäuse**)

mehrere *several*

das Programm *program* (pl. **die Programme**)

speichern *to save*

die Tabellenkalkulation *spreadsheet analysis*
(pl. **die Tabellenkalkulationen**)

die Taste *key* (pl. **die Tasten**)

der Text *text* (pl. **die Texte**)

die Textverarbeitung *word processing*

unterstreichen *to underline* (**er hat unterstrichen**)

vorhin *a little while ago, earlier*

---

1. Ich schalte den Computer ein. Du hast den Computer vorhin ausgeschaltet.

---

2. Du hast auf die Taste gedrückt. Diese Taste fügt den Text ein.

---

3. Ich habe die Datei gespeichert. Ich habe die Datei bearbeitet.

   _____

4. Wir drucken die elektronische Post aus. Wir bekommen elektronische Post.

   _____

5. Ich muß den Dateinamen kopieren. Ich habe mir den Dateinamen ausgedacht.

   _____

6. Man muß ein Betriebssystem haben. Das Betriebssystem kann mehrere Programme laden.

   _____

7. Lies den Text! Der Text steht auf dem Bildschirm.

   _____

8. Öffnen Sie die Tabellenkalkulation! Wir haben gestern die Tabellenkalkulation gespeichert.

   _____

C. **Übersetzen Sie, bitte!** *(Please translate.)* Translate these sentence fragments that have relative clauses, based on each of the German sentences given. Notice that most of the English sentences drop the relative pronoun, which you will have to add in German.

1. Ich habe den Text bearbeitet.

   the text I edited _____

2. Wir haben die Datei geöffnet.

   the file we opened _____

3. Die Taste fügt Text ein.

   the key that pastes text _____

4. Hier benutzt man das Textverarbeitungsprogramm.

   the word-processing program one uses here

   _____

5. Du hast den Drucker eingeschaltet.

   the printer you turned on _____

   ➢➢➢➢➢

6. Er hat den Text ausgedruckt.

   the text he printed out _____

7. Wir müssen den Computer ausschalten.

   the computer we have to shut off _____

8. Dieses Ikon unterstreicht Wörter.

   the icon that underlines words _____

II. Relative Pronouns after Prepositions

■ In everyday English, prepositions in subordinate clauses are often placed at the end of a sentence:

This is the house that we lived in.

In German, however, prepositions in subordinate clauses must precede the relative pronoun.

Das ist das Haus, in dem wir gewohnt haben.

Prepositions do NOT contract with relative pronouns.

D. Früher. Frau Meier is showing her granddaughter around the house and neighborhood where she spent her childhood.

Beispiel Das ist das Viertel. Wir haben in diesem Viertel gewohnt.
➤ Das ist das Viertel, in dem wir gewohnt haben.

1. Wir kommen zu der Straße. Wir haben in dieser Straße gewohnt.

   _____

2. Hier ist der Garten. Ich habe in diesem Garten gespielt.

   _____

3. Das ist das Wohnzimmer. Wir haben uns in diesem Wohnzimmer unterhalten.

   _____

4. Hier ist der Tisch. Wir haben an diesem Tisch gegessen.

   _____

5. Siehst du die Schule? Ich bin in die Schule gegangen.

   _____

6. Hier ist der Metzger. Wir haben bei diesem Metzger Fleisch gekauft.

_____

7. Wir kommen zum Park. Wir sind jeden Tag in diesen Park gegangen.

_____

8. Ich will dir den See zeigen. Wir haben oft auf dem See gerudert.

_____

E. **Ein Stipendium.** *(A scholarship.)* Dieter's plans for the future depend on his getting a scholarship to Harvard. Combine each pair of sentences into a single sentence to find out whether he gets one.

Beispiel   Das Studium an der Universität ist teuer. Dieter will an dieser Universität studieren.
➤ Das Studium an der Universität, die Dieter besuchen will, ist teuer.

Die Universität

der Beamte *clerk, official* (pl. **die Beamten**)

sich bewerben um + acc. *to apply for*

bitten um + acc. *to ask for* (**er hat gebeten**)

erfordern *to require*

das Fach *subject* (pl. **die Fächer**)

<u>nach</u>**denken über** + acc. *to think over* (**er hat nachgedacht**)

das Seminar *specialized training; seminar* (pl. **die Seminare**)

sich immatrikulieren für *to register for*

das Stipendium *scholarship; financial aid*

<u>teil</u>**nehmen an** + dat. *to take part in* (**er hat teilgenommen**)

sich sorgen um *to worry about*

---

1. Geschichte ist das Fach. Dieters Freund will sich in diesem Fach immatrikulieren.

_____

2. Hier sind die Beamten. Er hat mit diesen Beamten über das Stipendium gesprochen.

_____

➤➤➤➤➤

3. Für ein Stipendium erfordert die Universität eine Prüfung. Dieter hat sich auf die Prüfung vorbereitet.

_____

4. Die Universität organisiert ein Seminar. Er hat an dem Seminar teilgenommen.

_____

5. Man hat ihm eine Liste von den Stipendien gegeben. Er kann sich um diese Stipendien bewerben.

_____

6. Das ist ein Plan. Er hat über diesen Plan viel nachgedacht.

_____

7. Das Studium ist die Sache. Er sorgt sich um die Sache.

_____

8. Der glückliche Dieter! Man hat ihm das Stipendium gegeben. Er hat um das Stipendium gebeten.

_____

III. The Narrative Past of *haben, sein,* and the Modals

■ German has, in addition to the perfect tense, a simple past tense related to English past tense forms such as *sang, ate, came, could,* etc. This tense is often called the *narrative past*. In everyday speech, these forms are infrequent, except for the simple tenses of **haben, sein,** and the modals. The simple past is similar in meaning to the perfect.

Study the simple past of **haben** and **sein**:

	singular	plural
first person	ich hatte	wir hatten
second person	du hattest	ihr hattet
third person	er/sie/es hatte	sie/Sie hatten

	singular	plural
first person	ich war	wir waren
second person	du warst	ihr wart
third person	er/sie/es war	sie/Sie waren

■ The past of the modals is formed by adding suffixes beginning with **t** to the stem:

	dürfen	**können**	**mögen**	**müssen**	**sollen**	**wollen**
ich	durfte	konnte	mochte	mußte	sollte	wollte
du	durftest	konntest	mochtest	mußtest	solltest	wolltest
er/sie/es	durfte	konnte	mochte	mußte	sollte	wollte
wir	durften	konnten	mochten	mußten	sollten	wollten
ihr	durftet	konntet	mochtet	mußtet	solltet	wolltet
sie/Sie	durften	konnten	mochten	mußten	sollten	wollten

The verb **wissen** *to know* has a similar past tense:

ich wußte, du wußtest, er wußte, wir wußten, ihr wußtet, sie wußten

F. Viele Probleme! *(Many problems!)* Rewrite the following story about a secretary's problems, changing all the verbs to the simple past.

Im Büro (At the office)

der Chef *boss* (pl. **die Chefs**; fem. **die Chefin**)

die Verschiebung *delay, postponement* (pl. **die Verschiebungen**)

---

1. Sie will den Brief schreiben.

   _____

2. Sie darf heute aber nicht zu lang im Büro bleiben.

   _____

3. Der Brief soll am Dienstag ankommen.

   _____

4. Sie hat viel Arbeit.

   _____

5. Sie kann ihn nicht schreiben.

   _____

6. Ihr Chef ist ihr böse.

   _____

➤➤➤➤➤

7. Er mag keine Verschiebungen.

_____

8. Er weiß nicht, daß sie so viel Arbeit hat.

_____

G. Nicht mehr. Answer each of these questions saying that what is asked about used to be so, but isn't any longer.

Beispiel   Haben sie noch einen Obst- und Gemüseladen?
     ➤ Sie hatten einen Obst- und Gemüseladen, aber sie haben ihn nicht mehr.

Nützliche Wörter

die Antwort *answer* (pl. **die Antworten**)

genug *enough*

der Obst- und Gemüseladen *fruit and vegetable store*
   (pl. **die Obst- und Gemüseläden**)

die Unterlage *document, official paper* (pl. **die Unterlagen**)

die Zeit *time*

---

1. Kannst du hier deutsche Zeitungen bekommen?

_____

2. Ist der Unterricht gut?

_____

3. Dürfen die Jungens ausgehen?

_____

4. Mögen die Kinder ihre Schule?

_____

5. Hast du die Unterlagen?

_____

6. Sollen sie sich heute treffen?

_____

7. Wußtet ihr die Antwort?

_____

8. Will sie mitkommen?

_____

H. Markus ist krank. Tell what happened when Markus was ill by changing the following sentences from perfect to simple past.

Beispiel   Markus hat Schnupfen gehabt.
   ➤ Markus hatte Schnupfen.

1. Er hat den Arzt anrufen sollen.

_____

2. Er hat ihn nicht anrufen wollen.

_____

3. Seine Mutter hat den Arzt anrufen müssen.

_____

4. Der Arzt hat sofort kommen können.

_____

5. Markus hat den Arzt nicht sehen mögen.

_____

6. Markus ist nicht zufrieden gewesen.

_____

7. Der Arzt hat gewußt, was Markus hat.

_____

8. Markus hat die Grippe gehabt.

_____

I. **Und du?** Answer the following questions in complete German sentences.

1. Hattest du diese Woche viel Arbeit? Konntest du alles fertigmachen?

   _____

2. Was solltest du und deine Freunde dieses Wochenende machen?

   _____

3. Um wieviel Uhr mußtest du heute in der Schule sein?

   _____

4. Welche Programme siehst du gern?

   _____

5. Welche Bücher oder Zeitschriften magst du?

   _____

J. **Aufsatz.** Pretend you are showing a friend around your town or around the place where you go on vacation. Describe the place using as many relative clauses as possible in sentences such as **Dort drüben siehst du den X, der . . . , Hier gibt es X, der. . . .** Write a paragraph of eight to ten sentences using the simple past where possible.

END VOCABULARY: GERMAN-ENGLISH

This vocabulary list includes all the German words presented in *Arbeitsheft*. For nouns, the gender is indicated by the definite article; plurals are given in parentheses. For verbs, irregular present tense forms and irregular past participles are given.

der	**Abend** evening; **zu Abend essen** to eat dinner			**auch** also
das	**Abendessen** dinner			**auch nicht** neither, not either
	aber however, but			**auf** on (+ *dat. or acc.*)
	abfahren to depart, leave (**ist abgefahren**)			**aufbauen** to set up (*a tent*)
	abholen to get, fetch (*a person or a thing*)			**aufführen** to perform
	abreisen to set out on a trip (**ist abgereist**)	die	**Aufgabe** assignment; homework (*pl.* **die Aufgaben**)
der	**Absatz** paragraph (*pl.* **die Absätze**)			**aufhängen** to hang up (**er hängt auf, hat aufgehängt**)
	abschließen to finish (**hat abgeschlossen**)			**aufhören** to stop
	abstellen to turn off			**aufmachen** to open
	acht eight	die	**Aufnahme** picture, photo (*pl.* **die Aufnahmen**); **Aufnahmen machen** to take pictures
	achtzehn eighteen			**aufnehmen** to record (**er nimmt auf, hat aufgenommen**)
	achtzig eighty			**aufräumen** to clean up, straighten up
die	**Ahnung** idea (*pl.* **die Ahnungen**)	der	**Aufsatz** composition (*pl.* **die Aufsätze**)
die	**Akte** file, record (*pl.* **die Akten**)			**aufstehen** to get up (**ist aufgestanden**)
die	**Aktentasche** briefcase (*pl.* **die Aktentaschen**)			**aufwachen** to wake up (**ist aufgewacht**)
	alle all, everyone (*takes plural verb*)			**aus** out of (+ *dat.*)
die	**Allee** avenue (*pl.* **die Alleen**)	die	**Ausbildung** education, training
	alles everything	sich	**ausdenken** (+ *acc.*) to think up (**hat sich ausgedacht**)
	als when (*refers to a single event in the past*)			**ausdrucken** to print out
	alt old			**ausgeben** to spend money (**er gibt aus, hat ausgegeben**)
	an at, on, against (+ *dat. or acc.*)			**ausgehen** to go out (*on a date, for an evening*) (**ist ausgegangen**)
das	**Andenken** souvenir (*pl.* **die Andenken**)	das	**Ausland** foreign country; **im Ausland** abroad
	ander other	der	**Ausländer** foreigner
	ändern to change			**auspacken** to unpack
	anders else	sich	**ausruhen** to rest
	angeln to fish			**ausschalten** to switch off
der/die	**Angestellte** employee (*pl.* **die Angestellten**)			**aussehen** to look like (**er sieht aus, hat ausgesehen**)
	Angst haben to be afraid			**außer** except (+ *dat.*)
	anhalten to stop (**hat angehalten**)			**aussteigen** to get off (**ist ausgestiegen**)
sich	**anhören** (+ *acc.*) to listen to			**austauschen** to exchange
	ankommen to arrive (**ist angekommen**)			**ausziehen** to take off article of clothing (**hat ausgezogen**); **sich ausziehen** to get undressed (**hat sich ausgezogen**)
sich	**ansehen** (+ *acc.*) to have a look at, watch (**hat sich angesehen**)	das	**Auto** car (*pl.* **die Autos**)
	anstellen to turn on			**Auto fahren** to drive
die	**Antwort** answer (*pl.* **die Antworten**)			
	antworten to answer	das	**Baby** baby
sich	**anziehen** to get dressed (**hat sich angezogen**)			**backen** to bake (**er bäckt, hat gebacken**)
der	**Anzug** suit (*pl.* **die Anzüge**)	der	**Bäcker** baker (*pl.* **die Bäcker**)
	anzünden to light, kindle	die	**Bäckerin** baker
der	**Apfel** apple (*pl.* **die Äpfel**)	der	**Badeanzug** bathing suit (*pl.* **die Badeanzüge**)
das	**Apfelmuß** applesauce	das	**Badezimmer** bathroom
die	**Arbeit** work	der	**Bahnhof** railroad station (*pl.* **die Bahnhöfe**)
	arbeiten to work			**bald** right away, immediately
der	**Arbeiter** worker (*pl.* **die Arbeiter**)	die	**Bank** bank (*pl.* **die Banken**)
die	**Arbeiterin** worker			**Bauchschmerzen haben** to have a stomachache
das	**Arbeitszimmer** study			**bauen** to build
der	**Architekt** architect (*pl.* **die Architekten**)	die	**Baustelle** construction site
die	**Architektin** architect			
	ärgerlich annoying			
	ärgern to annoy, irritate			
der	**Arm** arm (*pl.* **die Arme**)			
	arm poor			
	artig good, well-behaved (*said of children*)			
der	**Artikel** article			
der	**Arzt** doctor (*pl.* **die Ärzte**)			
die	**Ärztin** doctor			

der   **Beamte** clerk, official (*pl.* **die Beamten**)

  beantworten: eine Frage beantworten
    to answer a question

  bearbeiten to edit

  bedauern to regret, be sorry about

  bedeuten to mean, signify

sich   **beeilen** to hurry

  begabt talented

  begleiten to accompany

  begrüßen to greet

  bei by, at, at the house of (+ *dat.*)

  beige beige

das   **Bein** leg (*pl.* **die Beine**)

  beißen to bite (**hat gebissen**)

  bekommen to get, receive (**hat bekommen**)

  beliebt popular

sich   **benehmen** to behave (**er benimmt sich, hat sich benommen**)

  benutzen to use

  bequem comfortable

der   **Berg** mountain (*pl.* **die Berge**)

der   **Bericht** report

der   **Berufsberater** career counselor

die   **Berufswelt** the world of professions and occupations

  berühmt famous

sich   **beschäftigen mit** to occupy oneself with

die   **Beschäftigung** activity

  beschließen to decide (**hat beschlossen**)

  beschneiden to prune, cut back (**hat beschnitten**)

  beschreiben to describe (**hat beschrieben**)

  besichtigen: die Stadt besichtigen to tour the city

  besonder special

  besprechen to discuss (**er bespricht, hat besprochen**)

die   **Besserung** improvement, recovery (*pl.* **die Besserungen**)

  bestellen to order

  besuchen to visit

der   **Betrieb** company, factory (*pl.* **die Betriebe**)

das   **Betriebssystem** operating system (*pl.* **die Betriebssysteme**)

das   **Bett** bed (*pl.* **die Betten**)

  bevor before

sich   **bewerben um** (+ *acc.*) to apply for

  bezahlen to pay

  bezweifeln to doubt

die   **Bibliothek** library (*pl.* **die Bibliotheken**)

das   **Bild** picture (*pl.* **die Bilder**)

der   **Bildschirm** screen (*pl.* **die Bildschirme**)

  billig cheap

  binden to tie (**hat gebunden**); **einen Knoten binden** to tie a knot

  bis until, up to (+ *acc.*)

  bitten um (+ *acc.*) to ask for (**hat gebeten**)

  bitter bitter

  blau blue

  bleiben to remain, stay (**ist geblieben**)

der   **Block** pad of paper (*pl.* **die Blocks** *or* **Blöcke**)

  blöd dumb

die   **Blume** flower

die   **Bluse** blouse (*pl.* **die Blusen**)

der   **Boden** floor

die   **Bonbons** (*pl.*) candy

  böse angry; **böse sein** + *dat.* to be angry with someone

  brauchen to need

  braun brown

  brechen to break (**er bricht, hat gebrochen**); **sich den Arm brechen** to break one's arm

  breit wide

das   **Brennholz** firewood

der   **Brief** letter (*pl.* **die Briefe**)

die   **Briefmarke** (*pl.* **die Briefmarken**) postage stamp

  bringen to bring (**hat gebracht**)

das   **Brot** bread

die   **Brücke** bridge

das   **Buch** book (*pl.* **die Bücher**)

das   **Bücherregal** bookcase (*pl.* **die Bücherregale**)

die   **Buchhandlung** bookstore (*pl.* **die Buchhandlungen**)

  bügeln to iron

  bummeln to stroll; **einen Schaufensterbummel machen** to go window-shopping

  bunt colorful

das   **Büro** office

der   **Bus** bus (*pl.* **die Busse**)

der   **Busbahnhof** bus station

der   **CD-Spieler** CD player (*pl.* **die CD-Spieler**)

der   **Chemiker** chemist (*pl.* **die Chemiker**)

die   **Chemikerin** chemist

das   **Comicbuch** comic book (*pl.* **die Comicbücher**)

der   **Computer** computer (*pl.* **die Computer**)

der   **Dachboden** attic (*pl.* **die Dachböden**)

  danach afterwards

  dann then

  das that

die   **Datei** file (*pl.* **die Dateien**)

  decken to cover; to set (*the table*)

  dein your

  dekorieren to decorate

das   **Deutschland** Germany

die   **Deutschstunde** German class

der   **Dienstag** Tuesday; **am Dienstag** on Tuesday; **dienstags** on Tuesdays

  dir to/for you

die   **Diskette** diskette

der   **Dom** cathedral (*pl.* **die Dome**)

die   **Donau** Danube (*River*)

der   **Donnerstag** Thursday; **am Donnerstag** on Thursday; **donnerstags** on Thursdays

  dort drüben over there

  dort unten down there

die   **Dose** can (*pl.* **die Dosen**)

  drei three

  dreißig thirty

  dreizehn thirteen

  drücken to press; **eine Taste drücken** to press a key

der   **Drucker** printer (*pl.* **die Drucker**)

  du you (*informal singular*)

dumm stupid
dunkel dark
dunkelblau dark blue
durch through (+ *acc.*)
dürfen may, to be allowed to (**ich darf**)
Durst haben to be thirsty
sich **duschen** to take a shower

ein a
einfügen to paste (*in word processing*)
eingehen to arrive, be received (*letters, faxes, notices*)
einhundert one hundred
einige some
sich **einigen** auf + *acc.* to agree on
einkaufen to shop, to shop for
einladen to invite (**er lädt ein, hat eingeladen**)
einpacken to pack
eins one
einschalten to switch on
einschlafen to fall asleep (**ist eingeschlafen**)
einschlagen to choose (*a career, a course of study*)
einsperren to lock up
einsteigen to get in, get on (*a vehicle*) (**ist eingestiegen**)
die **Eintrittskarte** ticket (*pl.* **die Eintrittskarten**)
der **Einwohner** inhabitant (*pl.* **die Einwohner**)
das **Eis** ice cream
das **Eisen** iron
das **elektrische Gerät** electrical appliance (*pl.* **die elektrischen Geräte**)
die **elektronische Post** e-mail
elf eleven
der **Ellbogen** elbow (*pl.* **die Ellbogen**)
empfehlen to recommend
sich **entscheiden für** to decide (**hat sich entschieden**)
sich **entspannen** to relax
er he
das **Ereignis** event (*pl.* **die Ereignisse**)
erfordern to require
sich **erholen** to recover
sich **erkälten** to catch cold
erklären to explain
erledigen to take care of (*chores, errands*)
sich **ernähren** to nourish oneself, eat
erreichen to contact, reach
erwarten to expect
erzählen to tell, recount
die **Erzählung** story (*pl.* **die Erzählungen**)
erzeugen to produce
essen to eat (**er ißt, hat gegessen**)
das **Essen** food
das **Eßzimmer** dining room
etwas something; **etwas anderes** something else
euch to/for you; you
euer your

das **Fach** subject (*pl.* **die Fächer**)
fähig capable, skillful
das **Fahrrad** bicycle (*pl.* **die Fahrräder**)

fallen to fall (**er fällt, ist gefallen**)
falsch verbunden sein to have the wrong number
die **Familie** family
die **Farbe** color (*pl.* **die Farben**)
faul lazy
das **Fax** fax (*pl.* **die Faxe**)
fegen to sweep
fehlen: in der Schule fehlen to be absent from school
der **Fehler** mistake (*pl.* **die Fehler**)
feiern to celebrate
das **Fenster** window (*pl.* **die Fenster**)
fernsehen to watch television (**hat ferngesehen**)
der **Fernseher** TV set (*pl.* **die Fernseher**)
fertig ready
fertigmachen to finish
fesch stylish, smart
der **Film** film, movie (*pl.* **die Filme**)
der **Finger** finger (*pl.* **die Finger**)
der **Fisch** fish
die **Flasche** bottle (*pl.* **die Flaschen**)
das **Fleisch** meat
fleißig hard-working
fliegen to fly (**ist geflogen**)
der **Flug** flight (*pl.* **die Flüge**)
der **Flughafen** airport (*pl.* **die Flughäfen**)
das **Flugzeug** airplane (*pl.* **die Flugzeuge**)
der **Fluß** river (*pl.* **die Flüsse**)
folgen to follow
das **Foto** photo, picture (*pl.* **die Fotos**)
der **Fotoapparat** camera (*pl.* **die Fotoapparate**)
die **Fotografie** photo (*pl.* **die Fotografien**)
der **Fotokopierer** photocopier (*pl.* **die Fotokopierer**)
Fotos machen to take pictures
Fragen stellen to ask questions
die **Frau** wife, woman; Mrs. (*pl.* **die Frauen**)
frei free; **einen freien Tag haben** to have a day off
der **Freitag** Friday; **am Freitag** on Friday; **freitags** on Fridays
der **Fremdenverkehr** tourism
sich **freuen** to be glad; **sich freuen über** + *acc.* to be happy about; **es freut mich, daß** I'm glad that
der **Freund** friend (*pl.* **die Freunde**)
die **Freundin** friend
freundlich friendly, in a friendly manner
frisch fresh
froh happy
fröhlich cheerful
früher before, earlier
das **Frühstück** breakfast
sich **wohl fühlen** to feel good
fünf five
fünfzehn fifteen
fünfzig fifty
für for (+ *acc.*)
der **Fuß** foot (*pl.* **die Füße**)
das **Fußballspiel** soccer (*pl.* **die Fußballspiele**)
das **Fußballstadion** soccer stadium (*pl.* **die Fußballstadien**)

die   **Fußgängerzone** pedestrian-only zone
     (*pl.* **die Fußgängerzonen**)
     füttern to feed

die   **ganze Woche** all week, the entire week
den   **ganzen Monat** all month, the entire month
den   **ganzen Tag** all day long
der   **Garten** garden (*pl.* **die Gärten**)
der   **Gärtner** gardener (*pl.* **die Gärtner**)
die   **Gärtnerin** gardener
der   **Gast** guest (*pl.* **die Gäste**)
das   **Gebäude** building (*pl.* **die Gebäude**)
     geben to give (**er gibt, hat gegeben**); **es gibt**
     there is, there are
die   **Geburtsstadt** native city
     (*pl.* **die Geburtsstädte**)
der   **Geburtstag** birthday (*pl.* **die Geburtstage**)
der   **Gedanke** thought (*pl.* **die Gedanken**)
das   **Gedicht** poem (*pl.* **die Gedichte**)
     gefallen to please; to like (*used with dative of person*) (**hat gefallen**); **es gefällt mir, daß**
     I'm pleased that
     gegenüber across from, opposite (+ *dat.*)
     gehen to go
     gehorchen to obey (+ *dat.*)
     gehören to belong to (+ *dat.*)
     gehorsam obedient
     gelb yellow
das   **Geld** money
das   **Gemälde** painting (*pl.* **die Gemälde**)
das   **Gemüse** vegetables
     genau precise
     genug enough
das   **Gepäck** luggage
     gerade just, just now
     geradeaus straight ahead
das   **Geschäft** shop, store (*pl.* **die Geschäfte**)
die   **Geschäftsfrau** businesswoman
     (*pl.* **die Geschäftsfrauen**)
der   **Geschäftsmann** businessman
     (*pl.* **die Geschäftsleute**)
das   **Geschenk** gift (*pl.* **die Geschenke**)
die   **Geschichte** story (*pl.* **die Geschichten**)
     geschickt capable, skillful
das   **Geschirr** dishes
das   **Gespräch** conversation (*pl.* **die Gespräche**)
das   **Getränk** drink (*pl.* **die Getränke**)
     gießen to water
das   **Glas** glass (*pl.* **die Gläser**)
     glauben to believe
     gliedern to divide
     gratulieren: zum Geburtstag gratulieren
       to congratulate someone (*on the occasion of his or her birthday*)
     grau gray
die   **Grippe** flu
     groß big, large
die   **Großmutter** grandmother
     (*pl.* **die Großmütter**)
der   **Großvater** grandfather (*pl.* **die Großväter**)
     grün green
     grüßen to greet, say hello to
der   **Gürtel** belt (*pl.* **die Gürtel**)

das   **Haar** (*a single*) hair (*pl.* **die Haare**)
     haben (*irreg.*) to have
das   **Hähnchen** chicken
der   **Handschuh** glove (*pl.* **die Handschuhe**)
die   **Harke** rake (*pl.* **die Harken**)
     häßlich ugly
     Haupt- (*prefix*) main
die   **Hauptstadt** capital (*pl.* **die Hauptstädte**)
die   **Hausarbeit** housework
die   **Hausaufgaben** (pl.) homework; **Hausaufgaben aufgeben** to give homework
das   **Heft** notebook (*pl.* **die Hefte**)
     Heimweh haben to be homesick
     heiß hot
     heißen to be called, be named
     helfen to help (+ *dat.*) (**er hilft, hat geholfen**)
     hell light
     hellblau light blue
das   **Hemd** shirt (*pl.* **die Hemden**)
     herausnehmen to take out
der   **Herd** cooking stove (*pl.* **die Herde**)
     herkommen to come here
     herunterladen to download
     heute today
     heute in einer Woche a week from today
     hinter behind (+ *dat.* or *acc.*)
     hoch high
     hoffen to hope
     höflich polite
     holen to get
     hören to hear
der   **Hörsaal** lecture hall (*pl.* **die Hörsäle**)
die   **Hose** pair of pants (*pl.* **die Hosen**)
das   **Hotel** hotel (*pl.* **die Hotels**)
     hübsch pretty
der   **Hund** dog (*pl.* **die Hunde**)
     hundert hundred
     Hunger haben to be hungry

     ich I
die   **Idee** idea (*pl.* **Ideen**)
     ihm to/for him, it
     ihnen to/for them
     Ihnen to/for you (*formal*)
     ihr her; to/for her; **ihr-** their
     ihr you (*informal pl.*)
     Ihr your (*formal*)
das   **Ikon** icon (*pl.* **die Ikonen**)
die   **Imbißstube** snack bar (*pl.* **die Imbißstuben**)
sich   **immatrikulieren an** to register for
     immer always
     in in (+ *dat.* or *acc.*)
     in der Nähe nearby
die   **Industrie** industry (*pl.* **die Industrien**)
die   **Informatik** computer science
der   **Ingenieur** engineer (*pl.* **die Ingenieure**)
die   **Ingenieurin** engineer
das   **Institut** institute (*pl.* **die Institute**)
     interessant interesting
sich   **interessieren für** to be interested in
     irgendwo hier somewhere around here
     irgendwohin (*in the direction of*) somewhere,
       anywhere

die **Jacke** jacket (*pl.* **die Jacken**)
die **Jeans** (*pl.*) jeans
    jede Woche every week
    jeden Monat every month
    jeden Tag every day
    jemand someone, somebody
    jetzt now
die **Jugendherberge** youth hostel
    (*pl.* **die Jugendherbergen**)
    jung young

der **Kaffee** coffee
das **Kalbfleisch** veal
    kalt cold
sich **kämmen** *or* **sich die Haare kämmen** to comb
    one's hair
    kaputt broken, out of order
die **Kartoffel** potato (*pl.* **die Kartoffeln**)
der **Käse** cheese
der **Kassettenrekorder** tape recorder
    (*pl.* **die Kassettenrekorder**)
die **Katze** cat (*pl.* **die Katzen**)
    kauen to chew
    kaufen to buy
das **Kaufhaus** department store
    (*pl.* **die Kaufhäuser**)
der **Kaufmann** businessman (*pl.* **die Kaufleute**)
der **Kaugummi** chewing gum
    kehren to sweep
    kein no
der **Keller** cellar, basement (*pl.* **die Keller**)
der **Kellner** waiter (*pl.* **die Kellner**)
die **Kellnerin** waitress
der **Kerl** fellow (*pl.* **die Kerle** *or* **die Kerls**)
das **Kind** child (*pl.* **die Kinder**)
das **Kino** movie theater (*pl.* **die Kinos**)
der **Kiosk** newsstand (*pl.* **die Kioske**)
die **Kirche** church (*pl.* **die Kirchen**)
    klagen to complain
das **Klassenzimmer** classroom
    (*pl.* **die Klassenzimmer**)
das **Kleid** dress (*pl.* **die Kleider**)
die **Kleider** (*pl.*) clothing
    klein small
    klingeln to ring
    klug intelligent, clever
das **Knie** knee (*pl.* **die Knie**)
der **Knöchel** ankle (*pl.* **die Knöchel**)
der **Knochen** bone (*pl.* **die Knochen**)
    kochen to cook
der **Koffer** suitcase (*pl.* **die Koffer**)
    kommen to come
    können can, be able to (**ich kann**)
sich **konzentrieren auf** (+ *acc.*) to concentrate on
das **Konzert** concert (*pl.* **die Konzerte**)
    Kopfschmerzen haben to have a headache
    kopieren to copy
der **Körper** body (*pl.* **die Körper**)
    korrigieren to correct
    kosten to cost
    köstlich delicious
    kräftig strong
das **Krankenhaus** hospital (*pl.* **die Krankenhäuser**)

der **Krankenpfleger** male nurse
    (*pl.* **die Krankenpfleger**)
die **Krankenschwester** nurse
    (*pl.* **die Krankenschwestern**)
die **Krawatte** necktie (*pl.* **die Krawatten**)
die **Küche** kitchen (*pl.* **die Küchen**)
der **Kuchen** cake (*pl.* **die Kuchen**)
der **Kugelschreiber** ballpoint pen
    kühl cool
der **Kuli** ballpoint pen
sich **kümmern um** (+ *acc.*) to take care of
der **Künstler** artist (*pl.* **die Künstler**)
die **Künstlerin** artist
das **Kunstmuseum** art museum
    (*pl.* **die Kunstmuseen**)
    kürzen to shorten
die **Kusine** female cousin (*pl.* **die Kusinen**)

das **Labor** laboratory (*pl.* **die Labors**)
    lächeln to smile
    lachen to laugh
der **Laden** store (*pl.* **die Läden**)
    laden to load (**er lädt, hat geladen**)
die **Lage** situation (*pl.* **die Lagen**)
das **Laken** bedsheet (*pl.* **die Laken**)
die **Lampe** lamp (*pl.* **die Lampen**)
das **Land** country; German state (*pl.* **die Länder**)
    lang long
sich **langweilen** to be bored
    langweilig boring
der **Lärm** noise
    lassen to let, allow (**er läßt, hat gelassen**)
die **Laufbahn** career (*pl.* **die Laufbahnen**)
    laut loud
    leben to live, be alive
    lecker tasty, delicious
    legen to put into a reclining or horizontal
    position; **sich zu Bett legen** to go
    to bed
der **Lehrer** teacher (*pl.* **die Lehrer**)
die **Lehrerin** teacher
das **Lehrerzimmer** staff room
    leicht easy
    leihen to lend (**er lieh, hat geliehen**)
    lernen to learn, study
    lesen to read (**er liest, hat gelesen**)
    leserlich legible
der **Leuchtstift** highlighter
das **Lied** song (*pl.* **die Lieder**)
die **Limonade** lemonade, soft drink
das **Lineal** ruler
    links to the left
die **Literatur** literature
    lösen: Eintrittskarten lösen to buy tickets
    lustig funny

    machen to make, do
    mähen to cut, mow
    manchmal sometimes
der **Mann** husband, man
der **Mantel** coat (*pl.* **die Mäntel**)
das **Märchen** fairy tale
die **Mark** mark (*unit of currency in Germany*)

der	**Markt** market (*pl.* **die Märkte**)		**nötig** necessary; **es ist nötig/notwendig, daß**
der	**Marktplatz** marketplace		it's necessary that
	(*pl.* **die Marktplätze**)	die	**Notizen** notes
die	**Maus** mouse (*pl.* **die Mäuse**)		
	mehrere several	der	**Obst- und Gemüseladen** fruit and vegetable
	mein my		store (*pl.* **die Obst- und Gemüseläden**)
	meinen to think, be of the opinion of		**offen** open
die	**Mensa** cafeteria		**öffnen** to open
der	**Mensch** human being (*pl.* **die Menschen**)		**oft** often
der	**Metzger** butcher (*pl.* **die Metzger**)		**ohne** without (+ *acc.*)
die	**Metzgerin** butcher	die	**Oma** Grandma (*pl.* **die Omas**)
die	**Milch** milk	der	**Onkel** uncle (*pl.* **die Onkel**)
die	**Minute** minute (*pl.* **die Minuten**)	der	**Opa** Grandpa (*pl.* **die Opas**)
	mir to/for me	die	**Oper** opera (*pl.* **die Opern**)
	mit with (+ *dat.*)		**orange** orange
	mitbringen to bring along	der	**Orangensaft** orange juice
	mitkommen to come along	das	**Österreich** Austria
	mitnehmen to take along		
das	**Mittagessen** lunch	das	**Paket** package (*pl.* **die Pakete**)
der	**Mittwoch** Wednesday; **am Mittwoch**	die	**Panne** flat tire; **eine Panne haben** to have
	on Wednesday; **mittwochs** on Wednesdays		a flat tire
	möchte would like	das	**Papier** paper (*pl.* **die Papiere**)
	modern modern	der	**Papierkorb** wastepaper basket
	modisch fashionable		(*pl.* **die Papierkörbe**)
	mögen to like (**ich mag**)	der	**Park** park (*pl.* **die Parks**)
	möglich possible; **es ist möglich, daß**	der	**Passagier** passenger (*pl.* **die Passagiere**)
	it's possible that		**pauken** to cram, study hard
der	**Monat** month (*pl.* **die Monate**)	der	**Pianist** pianist (*pl.* **die Pianisten**)
der	**Montag** Monday; **am Montag** on Monday;	der	**Pinsel** paintbrush (*pl.* **die Pinsel**)
	montags on Mondays	die	**Pizza** pizza (*pl.* **die Pizzas**)
	morgen tomorrow	der	**Plan** plan (*pl.* **die Pläne**)
	müde tired	der	**Platz** place (*pl.* **die Plätze**)
der	**Müll** garbage, trash		**Platz nehmen** to take a seat
das	**Museum** museum (*pl.* **die Museen**)		**plaudern** to chat
	müssen must, have to (**ich muß**)	der	**Polizist** policeman (*pl.* **die Polizisten**)
die	**Mutter** mother (*pl.* **die Mütter**)	die	**Polizistin** policewoman
		die	**Post** mail; post office (*pl.* **die Posten**)
	nach to; after (+ *dat.*)		**prellen** to bruise; **sich das Knie prellen**
der	**Nachbar** neighbor (*pl.* **die Nachbarn**)		to bruise one's knee
	nachdem after	das	**Programm** program (*pl.* **die Programme**)
	nachdenken über (+ *acc.*) to think over	der	**Programmierer** programmer
	(**er hat nachgedacht**)		(*pl.* **die Programmierer**)
	nachfragen to inquire about	die	**Programmiererin** programmer
	nächst- next	die	**Prüfung** test (*pl.* **die Prüfungen**)
die	**Nähe** proximity; **in der Nähe** near, close by	der	**Pulli** sweater (*pl.* **die Pullis**)
	nähen to sew		**putzen** to clean; to shine (*shoes*); **sich die Zähne**
sich	**nähern** (+ *dat.*) to approach, come close to		**putzen** to brush one's teeth
das	**Nahrungsmittel** food, nourishment		
der	**Name** name (**dem/den Namen**;		**Rad fahren** (*or* **radfahren**) to ride a bicycle,
	pl. **die Namen**)		go bicycle riding
	naß wet	der	**Radiergummi** eraser
	neben near; next to (+ *dat. or acc.*)	das	**Radio** radio (*pl.* **die Radios**)
	nett nice, pleasant	der	**Rasen** lawn
	neu new	sich	**rasieren** to shave
	neun nine	der	**Rat** piece of advice (*pl.* **die Ratschläge**)
	neunzehn nineteen		**raten** to advise
	neunzig ninety	das	**Rathaus** city hall
	nicht weit weg not far away		**rechnen** to calculate, compute
	nichts nothing		**rechts** to the right
	niedrig low	der	**Rechtsanwalt** lawyer (*pl.* **die Rechtsanwälte**)
	niemals never	die	**Rechtsanwältin** lawyer
	niemand no one, nobody		**reden** to speak, talk
die	**Note** mark, grade (*pl.* **die Noten**)	der	**Regenschirm** umbrella (*pl.* **die Regenschirme**)

	reich rich	
	reichen to pass something at the table; to hand	
der	**Reis** rice	
das	**Reisebüro** travel agency (*pl.* **die Reisebüros**)	
der	**Reisebürokaufmann** travel agent (*pl.* **die Reisebürokaufleute**)	
der	**Reiseführer** guidebook (*pl.* **die Reiseführer**)	
der	**Reiseleiter** tour guide (*pl.* **die Reiseleiter**)	
die	**Reiseleiterin** tour guide	
	reisen to travel (**ist gereist**)	
der	**Reisepaß** passport (*pl.* **die Reisepässe**)	
die	**Reiseroute** itinerary (*pl.* **die Reiserouten**)	
	reiten to go horseback riding (**ist geritten**)	
	reparieren to repair, fix	
das	**Restaurant** restaurant (*pl.* **die Restaurants**)	
	riesig gigantic	
das	**Rindfleisch** beef	
der	**Ring** ring (*pl.* **die Ringe**)	
der	**Rock** skirt (*pl.* **die Röcke**)	
der	**Roman** novel (*pl.* **die Romane**)	
	rosa pink	
die	**Rose** rose (*pl.* **die Rosen**)	
	rot red	
der	**Rücken** back (*pl.* **die Rücken**)	
der	**Rucksack** day pack, backpack (*pl.* **die Rucksäcke**)	
	rudern to row	
	rufen to call (**hat gerufen**)	
sich	**ruhen** to rest	
	ruhig calm, quiet, peaceful	

die	**S-Bahn** high-speed railway (*pl.* **die S-Bahnen**)	
der	**Saft** juice (*pl.* **die Säfte**)	
	sagen to say	
das	**Salz** salt	
	salzig salty	
	sammeln to collect; to gather	
der	**Samstag** Saturday; **am Samstag** on Saturday; **samstags** on Saturdays	
der	**Sänger** singer (*pl.* **die Sänger**)	
die	**Sängerin** singer	
die	**Satellitenschüssel** satellite dish (*pl.* **die Satellitenschüsseln**)	
	sauber clean	
	sauer sour	
die	**Schachtel** box (*pl.* **die Schachteln**)	
	schaden to harm	
	scharf spicy	
die	**Schaufel** shovel (*pl.* **die Schaufeln**)	
	schenken to give as a gift	
	schick smart-looking	
	schicken to send	
das	**Schiff** ship (*pl.* **die Schiffe**)	
der	**Schinken** ham	
	schlafen to sleep (**hat geschlafen**); **schlafen gehen** to go to bed	
der	**Schlafsack** sleeping bag (*pl.* **die Schlafsäcke**)	
das	**Schlafzimmer** bedroom (*pl.* **die Schlafzimmer**)	
	schlecht bad	
	schließen to close (**hat geschlossen**)	
	schließlich finally	
	Schlittschuh laufen to ice skate	
das	**Schloß** castle	

	schmal narrow	
	schmutzig dirty	
	schneiden to cut, slice (**hat geschnitten**); **in Stücke schneiden** to cut apart, into pieces	
der	**Schnellzug** express train (*pl.* **die Schnellzüge**)	
das	**Schnitzel** breaded cutlet (*pl.* **die Schnitzel**)	
	Schnupfen haben to have a cold	
	schon already	
	schön beautiful	
der	**Schrank** closet, cupboard (*pl.* **die Schränke**)	
	schreiben to write (**hat geschrieben**)	
der	**Schreibtisch** desk (*pl.* **die Schreibtische**)	
	schreien to scream, shout (**hat geschrien**)	
der	**Schriftsteller** author (*pl.* **die Schriftsteller**)	
die	**Schriftstellerin** author	
die	**Schublade** drawer (*pl.* **die Schubladen**)	
der	**Schuh** shoe (*pl.* **die Schuhe**)	
	schulden to owe	
die	**Schule** school (pl. **die Schulen**)	
der	**Schüler** student (*pl.* **die Schüler**)	
die	**Schülerin** student	
der	**Schulhof** schoolyard, playground (*pl.* **die Schulhöfe**)	
die	**Schultasche** school bag (*pl.* **die Schultaschen**)	
	schwach weak	
	schwarz black	
die	**Schweiz** Switzerland	
	schwierig difficult	
das	**Schwimmbad** swimming pool (*pl.* **die Schwimmbäder**)	
	sechs six	
	sechzehn sixteen	
	sechzig sixty	
der	**See** lake (*pl.* **die Seen**)	
	segeln to sail	
	sein his, its	
	sein to be (**ist gewesen**)	
	seit since (+ *dat.*)	
das	**Sekretariat** school office	
die	**Sekunde** second (*pl.* **die Sekunden**)	
das	**Seminar** specialized training; seminar (*pl.* **die Seminare**)	
der	**Sessel** armchair (*pl.* **die Sessel**)	
	setzen to place, put; **sich zu Tisch setzen** to sit down at the table	
die	**Shorts** (*pl.*) shorts	
	sicher sure	
	sie she, it; they	
	Sie you (*formal*)	
	sieben seven	
	siebzehn seventeen	
	siebzig seventy	
	singen to sing (**hat gesungen**)	
	sitzen to sit (**hat gesessen**)	
	Ski laufen to ski	
	sobald as soon as	
die	**Socke** sock (*pl.* **die Socken**)	
	sofort immediately	
der	**Sohn** son (*pl.* **die Söhne**)	
	sollen to be supposed to (**ich soll**)	
der	**Sonnabend** Saturday; **am Sonnabend** on Saturday; **sonnabends** on Saturdays	

sich	**sonnen** to sunbathe			**tanzen** to dance
der	**Sonntag** Sunday; **am Sonntag** on Sunday; **sonntags** on Sundays		der	**Taschenrechner** calculator (*pl.* **die Taschenrechner**)
sich	**sorgen um** to worry about		die	**Taste** key (*pl.* **die Tasten**)
der	**Spaß** joke; fun (*pl.* **die Späße**); **keinen Spaß verstehen** unable to take a joke			**tauchen** to go scuba diving
			der	**Tee** tea (*pl.* **die Tees**)
	spät late; **Wie spät ist es?** What time is it?			**teilnehmen an** (+ *dat.*) to participate in (**er nimmt teil, hat teilgenommen**)
	später later		das	**Telefon** telephone (*pl.* **die Telefone**)
	spazierengehen to walk, take a walk			**telefonisch** by phone
	speichern to save (*a computer file*)		der	**Teppich** carpet, rug (*pl.* **die Teppiche**)
die	**Speisekarte** menu (*pl.* **die Speisekarten**)			**teuer** expensive
das	**Spiel** game (*pl.* **die Spiele**)		der	**Text** text (*pl.* **die Texte**)
	spielen to play		die	**Textverarbeitung** word processing
das	**Spielzeug** toy (pl. **die Spielzeuge**)		das	**Theater** theater (*pl.* **die Theater**)
der	**Sport** physical education		der	**Tisch** table (*pl.* **die Tische**)
der	**Sportplatz** playing field (*pl.* **die Sportplätze**)		die	**Tochter** daughter (*pl.* **die Töchter**)
	sprechen to speak (**er spricht, hat gesprochen**)			**toll** great, terrific, awesome
die	**Spüle** sink (*pl.* **die Spülen**)		das	**Tonbandgerät** tape recorder (*pl.* **die Tonbandgeräte**)
	spülen to wash, rinse		der	**Topf** pot (*pl.* **die Töpfe**)
das	**Stadion** stadium (*pl.* **die Stadien**)			**traurig** sad
die	**Stadt** (*pl.* **die Städte**)		sich	**treffen** to meet, get together (*on an informal basis*) (**hat sich getroffen**)
der	**Stadtbummel** walk through town (*pl.* **die Stadtbummel**)			**trocken** dry
die	**Stadtmitte** center of town, downtown (*pl.* **die Stadtmitten**)			**trocknen** to dry; **sich trocknen** to dry oneself; **sich die Haare trocknen** to dry one's hair
das	**Stadtzentrum** downtown (*pl.* **die Stadtzentren**)			**tun** to do (**hat getan**)
der	**Stahl** steel		die	**Tür** door (*pl.* **die Türen**)
der	**Staub** dust		die	**Turnhalle** gymnasium (*pl.* **die Turnhallen**)
	staubsaugen to vacuum		der	**Turnschuh** sneaker (*pl.* **die Turnschuhe**)
	stecken to put inside of			**typisch** typical
	stellen to put, place (*in an upright position*)			
	sterben to die (**er stirbt, ist gestorben**)		die	**U-Bahn** subway (*pl.* **die U-Bahnen**)
die	**Stereoanlage** stereo system (*pl.* **die Stereoanlagen**)			**über** over (+ *dat. or acc.*)
der	**Stiefel** boot (*pl.* **die Stiefel**)		sich	**überlegen** to think about, reflect, consider
	still still, quiet			**übermorgen** day after tomorrow
das	**Stipendium** scholarship		die	**Übung** exercise, practice (*pl.* **die Übungen**)
	stoßen to push (**hat gestoßen**)		die	**Uhr** clock
der	**Strand** beach (*pl.* **die Strände**)			**um** around (+ *acc.*); **um die Ecke** around the corner; **um zwei Uhr** at two o'clock
die	**Straße** street (*pl.* **die Straßen**)			**unbequem** uncomfortable
die	**Straßenbahn** trolley (*pl.* **die Straßenbahnen**)			**ungefähr** approximately
das	**Streichholz** match (*pl.* **die Streichhölzer**)		das	**Unkraut** weed (*pl.* **die Unkräuter**); **Unkraut jäten** to weed
	streng strict			**unmöglich** impossible; **es ist unmöglich, daß** it's impossible that
der	**Strumpf** stocking (*pl.* **die Strümpfe**)			
der	**Student** student (*pl.* **die Studenten; dat.: dem Studenten**)			**uns** to/for us; us
				unser- our
die	**Studentin** student			**unter** under (+ *dat. or acc.*)
	studieren to study			**unterbrechen** to interrupt (**er unterbricht, hat unterbrochen**)
das	**Studium** studies, schooling (*pl.* **die Studien**)		sich	**unterhalten** to chat, converse (**er unterhält sich, hat sich unterhalten**)
der	**Stuhl** chair (*pl.* **die Stühle**)			
die	**Stunde** hour; class period (*pl.* **die Stunden**)		die	**Unterlage** document, official paper (*pl.* **die Unterlagen**)
	suchen to look for		der	**Unterricht** class, lessons
der	**Supermarkt** supermarket (*pl.* **die Supermärkte**)			**unterstreichen** to underline (**er hat unterstrichen**)
die	**Suppe** soup (*pl.* **die Suppen**)			
	surfen to go surfing		der	**Vater** father (*pl.* **die Väter**)
	süß sweet			**verärgern** to annoy
das	**T-Shirt** T-shirt (*pl.* **die T-Shirts**)			**verbessern** to improve
die	**Tabellenkalkulation** spreadsheet analysis (*pl.* **die Tabellenkalkulationen**)			
	täglich daily			
die	**Tante** aunt (*pl.* **die Tanten**)			

verboten forbidden; **es ist verboten, daß** it's forbidden to

verbringen to spend (*time*) (**hat verbracht**)

verbunden: falsch verbunden sein to have the wrong number

vergessen to forget (**er vergißt, hat vergessen**)

verkaufen to sell

der **Verkäufer** salesman (*pl.* **die Verkäufer**)

die **Verkäuferin** saleswoman

verlassen to leave (**er verläßt, hat verlassen**)

verletzen to injure; **sich verletzen** to hurt oneself; **sich das Bein verletzen** to hurt one's leg

verlieren to lose (**hat verloren**)

verpassen to miss (*an event, a train*)

verreist away, away on a trip

verschiedenartig various

verschwenden to waste

versprechen (*+ dat.*) to promise (**er verspricht, hat versprochen**)

verstauchen: sich den Knöchel verstauchen to sprain one's ankle

versuchen to try, attempt

vertragen to bear, stand (**er verträgt, hat vertragen**)

vertreten (**er vertritt, hat vertreten**): **sich den Fuß vertreten** to twist one's ankle

der/die **Verwandte** relative (*pl.* **die Verwandten**)

der **Vetter** male cousin (*pl.* **die Vettern**)

die **Videokamera** video camera (*pl.* **die Videokameras**)

der **Videorekorder** VCR (*pl.* **die Videorekorder**)

die **Videothek** video store (*pl.* **die Videotheken**)

viel a lot

vier four

das **Viertel** neighborhood (*pl.* **die Viertel**)

vierzehn fourteen

vierzig forty

von from, of (*+ dat.*)

vor in front of (*+ dat. or acc.*)

sich **vorbereiten auf morgen** to prepare oneself for tomorrow

vorhaben to plan, intend

vorhin a little while ago, earlier

der **Vorort** suburb (*pl.* **die Vororte**)

vorschlagen to suggest (**er schlägt vor, hat vorgeschlagen**)

wachsen to wax

wählen to choose

während during (*+ gen. or dat.*)

der **Wald** woods (*pl.* **die Wälder**)

die **Wand** wall (*pl.* **die Wände**)

wandern to hike

Wann? When?

warm warm

warten to wait; **warten auf** (*+ acc.*) to wait for

Warum? Why?

Was? What?

die **Wäsche** laundry

waschen to wash, do laundry (**er wäscht, hat gewaschen**); **sich waschen** to wash up; **sich die Haare waschen** to wash one's hair

der **Wäscheschrank** linen closet (*pl.* **die Wäscheschränke**)

wechseln to change (*money*)

wegfahren to drive off (**er fährt weg, ist weggefahren**)

weil because

weinen to cry

weiß white

weit weg far away

Wem? To/For whom?

Wen? Whom?

wenig little, not much

wenn when, if

Wer? Who?

werden to become (**du wirst, er wird, ist geworden**)

werfen to throw (**er wirft, hat geworfen**); **etwas auf den Boden werfen** to throw something on the floor

das **Werkzeug** tool (*pl.* **die Werkzeuge**)

Wessen? Whose?

wichtig important

Wie? How?

wir we

wischen to wipe

wissen to know (**er weiß, wußte, hat gewußt**)

die **Wissenschaft** science (*pl.* **die Wissenschaften**)

Wo? Where?

die **Woche** week (*pl.* **die Wochen**)

Wohin? Where to?

wohnen to live, reside

die **Wohnung** apartment (*pl.* **die Wohnungen**)

das **Wohnzimmer** living room (*pl.* **die Wohnzimmer**)

wollen to want (**ich will, wollte**)

wunderbar wonderful

wundern: es wundert mich, daß I'm surprised that

wünschen to wish

die **Wurst** sausage (*pl.* **die Würste**)

zahlen to pay

der **Zahn** tooth (*pl.* **die Zähne**)

der **Zahnarzt** dentist (*pl.* **die Zahnärzte**)

die **Zahnärztin** dentist

zehn ten

zeichnen to draw

zeigen to show

die **Zeit** time

die **Zeitschrift** magazine (*pl.* **die Zeitschriften**)

die **Zeitung** newspaper (*pl.* **die Zeitungen**)

das **Zelt** tent (*pl.* **die Zelte**)

zelten to go camping

der **Zeltplatz** campsite (*pl.* **die Zeltplätze**)

zerreißen to tear (**hat zerrissen**)

zerschneiden to cut up into pieces (**hat zerschnitten**)

zerstören to destroy

das **Zimmer** room (*pl.* **die Zimmer**)

zu to (*+ dat.*)

zu Fuß gehen to walk, go on foot

zu viel too much

zubereiten to prepare

der   **Zucker** sugar

    zufrieden satisfied, happy

der   **Zug** train (*pl.* **die Züge**)

    zuhören (+ *dat.*) to listen, pay attention to

    zuletzt finally, last thing

    zumachen to close

    zurückbringen to bring back
        (**hat zurückgebracht**)

    zurückfahren to drive back
        (**ist zurückgefahren**)

    zurückgeben to give back
        (**hat zurückgegeben**)

zurückgehen to go back (**ist zurückgegangen**)

zurückkommen to come back
    (**ist zurückgekommen**)

zusammenarbeiten to collaborate, cooperate
    (**hat zusammengearbeitet**)

zusammenkommen to get together (*on a more formal basis*) (**ist zusammengekommen**)

zwanzig twenty

zwei two

zweifelhaft doubtful

zwischen between (+ *dat. or acc.*)

zwölf twelve

INDEX